LaMar Boschman

Author of *The Rebirth of Music*

A HEART OF WORSHIP

*Experience a
Rebirth of Worship*

Foreword by Judson Cornwall

CREATION
HOUSE
BOOKS ABOUT SPIRIT-LED LIVING
ORLANDO, FLORIDA

Creation House
Strang Communications Company
600 Rinehart Road
Lake Mary, FL 32746
Web site: http://www.strang.com

Unless otherwise noted, all Scripture quotations are from the New
King James Version of the Bible. Copyright © 1979, 1980, 1982 by
Thomas Nelson Inc., publishers. Used by permission.

Scripture quotations marked AMP are from the Amplified Bible.
Old Testament copyright © 1965, 1987 by the Zondervan Corporation
The Amplified New Testament copyright © 1954, 1958, 1987 by the
Lockman Foundation. Used by permission.

Scripture quotations marked KJV are from the
King James Version of the Bible.

Scripture quotations marked NAS are from the New
American Standard Bible. Copyright © 1960, 1962, 1963,
1968, 1971, 1972, 1973, 1975, 1977 by the
Lockman Foundation. Used by permission.

Scripture quotations marked NEB are from the
New English Bible. Copyright © 1961, 1970 by the
Delegates of the Oxford University Press and the Syndics of the
Cambridge University Press. Used by permission.

Scripture quotations marked NIV are from the Holy Bible,
New International Version. Copyright © 1973, 1978, 1984,
International Bible Society. Used by permission.

Scripture quotations marked RSV are from the
Revised Standard Version of the Bible. Copyright © 1946,
1952, 1971 by the Division of Christian Education of the
National Council of the Churches of Christ in the USA
Used by permission.

First printing, May 1994
Second printing, August 1994
Third printing, February 1995
Fourth printing, October 1996
Fifth printing, February 1998

*To Pastor Carter and Ann Foster,
our friends and family
at Metroplex Covenant Church
in Colleyville, Texas.*

*We are on a journey in discovering
worship renewal. You have
blessed and inspired me.*

CONTENTS

Part II
Foundations of Worship

FOREWORD

WORSHIP IS a God-given urge we do not produce — nor can we deny it. This drive to worship is as genuine as the food-seeking drive. We are born with both of them, and they remain inherent in our natures from our birth until our burial. We can ignore them, but the penalties are severe. We can sublimate them, but they will rise up again and demand action. We can prostitute them, but that leaves the true craving unsatisfied. Or we can give them expression and find a full satisfaction.

Since we were born with a worship instinct, the problem has never been to find worshippers. The world is full of them. No explorer has ever found a tribe of people, however remote from civilization they may be, who did not worship. The problem has never been whether or not we will worship, but *whom* we will worship.

During this past decade there has been a revival of interest in worship. New forms of worship have been introduced, and we've enjoyed the rebirth of congregational participation. Many groups have replaced the hymnbooks with projectors and have removed the organ to make room for keyboards, drums, guitars and flutes. Vestments have been replaced with extremely casual clothes, and choirs have often been supplanted with a small number of singers with hand-held microphones. These have given a new expression to worship, but it is not "new" worship. Most of it is merely a recycling of prior forms of worship.

This fresh emphasis has stressed excellence in worship. Conferences have convened with the expressed purpose of helping to produce this excellence. Artists have taught less talented persons to create banners and flags. Gifted musicians have honed the skills of less trained instrumentalists. Successful leaders of worship have sought to teach less qualified persons how to inspire and motivate others to worship.

Much of this has been good, for God deserves the best we are capable of bringing to Him. As a traveling teacher, I can attest that the quality of our worship programs has taken giant steps forward during the past fifteen years, and I am grateful for this.

With this increased standard of performance by everyone who is involved in the worship program of the church, a sense has also come that what they are doing is worship. This is not necessarily so. That response may be melodious, but it is quite easy to sing or play instruments without worshipping — even if we play Christian music. The dance teams may release worship with body action, but they can also perform the finest choreographed dances in the most beautiful costumes without releasing worship. Worship is love responding to love. We do not initiate worship; we respond to it. Worship originates in God's great love for us. When we become aware of that love, our responses are worship responses, however crude or cultural they may be.

Throughout the Scriptures God has placed almost no emphasis on *how* we worship. Even a limited search will reveal the great variety of expressions of worship God accepts. Different cultures in the world respond differently, but none is penalized by God for being unique. He made them original. We need, therefore, to be careful lest we feel that our form of worship is *the* form of worship.

No, with God the issue is not *how* we worship but *whom* we worship. Here God is inflexible. Any worship that does not go directly to God the Father, God the Son or God the Spirit is patently classified as idolatry. Jesus told the woman at Jacob's well,

> The hour is coming, and now is, when the true worshipers will worship the Father in spirit and truth: for the Father is seeking such to worship Him (John 4:23).

Is the Father seeking worshippers? No! The world is full of them. Some worship their sports gods, other materialistic gods or gods of lust. God the Father is seeking true worshippers of Him. He demands a monopoly in this.

The issue of the moment, then, is not our method of worship or our skills in the performance of worship. It is the heart of worship that concerns God. Where are our minds when we extol God? Do our hearts really feel what our mouths proclaim during the seasons of worship?

The heart of a true worshipper does not need music, dancing, banners or congregational support to worship. When the heart reaches to God in worship, it is a very private and personal thing. These aids to worship can certainly assist in expression, but they rarely produce the worship. Pure worship comes out of a relationship with the living God. It is a response to an awareness of God's extended love.

LaMar Boschman has put his finger on the center of

worship in this book, *A Heart of Worship*. Although he is a skilled musician who has conducted many worship symposiums and conferences throughout the world, LaMar has reached beyond performance to the very Person of worship, the Lord Jesus Christ.

May God return His church to an involvement with Him. Worshipping Him as a loving God is the only way we will satisfy the innate drive to worship. Only as we see Him as greater will our worship become greater. ❦

Judson Cornwall
Phoenix, Arizona
January 1994

INTRODUCTION

I REMEMBER the first time I experienced wholehearted, Spirit-empowered worship. I was eighteen years old at the time and played bass in a Christian band we called the Lapels. The drummer had told me about a church that had a great choir, and the whole band decided to go and check it out. We went on a Sunday night, but the church was packed. You had to get there early to get a seat.

At seven o'clock the ushers cleared the aisles, and the latecomers had to wait in the foyer as the choir came marching in from the back of the sanctuary. Their purple robes flowed as they walked briskly to the tempo of the song they were singing. As they passed me down the two center aisles, I heard the harmony and felt a chill. Not only were they singing at the top of their voices and walking briskly, but they were clapping their hands. When they reached the front of the sanctuary, they filled the choir loft, and all 120 of them lifted 240 hands.

As a Mennonite, I was not used to many "amens" and "praise the Lords" in the middle of a worship service. Nor had I seen too many hands raised. I didn't know what all of this meant, but my heart started to race. I was nervous and awestruck all at the same time.

What amazed me was they were singing some of the same songs our band played. Yet there was something different about the way this group was singing them. They had a zeal, a joy, a flow of life that seemed supernatural.

I returned often to hear this "on fire" choir. Their spirit drew me back again and again. During one service I was sitting there in the middle of a pew with what seemed like a thousand others squeezed in around me. Suddenly the Lord impressed on me a verse I had read.

Lift up your hands in the sanctuary, and bless the Lord (Ps. 134:2).

I wrestled with that. First I said, "Lord, that is for the Pentecostals. They need that kind of emotional release."

Then I heard it louder in my spirit: "Lift *your* hands in the sanctuary, and bless the Lord."

I argued again, "I'm Mennonite. We don't do that."

The next time the Lord was firm with me: *"Lift your hands, and bless the Lord."*

I will never forget how hard it was for me to lift my hands that day. I was afraid everyone would look at me. But I knew I had to do it. So I lifted my right hand behind the head of the man in front of me and looked around to see if anyone noticed. No one seemed interested. So I raised it higher.

What a sensation! I felt as if I were going to fly. My spirit arose inside me. My whole body seemed lighter as I raised my arms over my head and reached my hands toward the ceiling. My burdens fell off. I was soaring inwardly.

Suddenly I *did* want everyone to see what I was doing. I looked around, but no one was noticing me, for they too had their hands and arms outstretched toward heaven. They were all singing their own praises to the Lord with their eyes closed.

What is happening here? I asked myself.

For several more years I wrestled with these different forms of worship. Is it biblical? Isn't this cultish? Why don't other churches worship like this? I had a thousand questions. Two things helped settle these issues for me.

1. This kind of worship was encouraged in the Scriptures.

2. When I participated in worship, there was life in it. It was real.

Ever-Flowering Devotion

I believe the Lord is leading the church into a new level of intimacy and urgency in worship. This rebirth of worship is centered around no single ministry or personality. It is the sovereign work of the Lord in the hearts of believing men and women. I want to encourage you to be a part of this tender, developing relationship between Christ and His bride.

Some of you may have tasted the joy that comes from expressing worship to our Savior. You are eager to learn more about expressing your worship. Others of you may wonder if you've ever truly worshipped the Lord, though you've participated dutifully in the church song service.

My desire in this book is to quicken your mind with tools that will bring your heart to a new level of vibrant, passionate worship. As you seek a rebirth of worship in your life, keep your focus on Jesus. The form or liturgy of worship may be visible to other people, but it does not determine the extent of one's worship. Worship is an attitude of the heart. And only the Lord can see that.

No one will ever be able to say, "I know everything about praise and worship." That is like saying, "I know how to love my wife." Only your wife can tell if in fact you know how to love her. Only she can answer the question: Does he express love to me?

We are all at different places in our worship. None of us has arrived, because Christianity is not a destination. It is a journey. And we'll never have complete knowledge and understanding of worship, though we can always keep learning.

Worship is like a flower that blossoms for a moment and then fades. Each flower is different and meaningful for the time that it exists, but a new flower must take its place when it is gone. So worship is not a goal but a life experience. It is an ever-flowering expression of sincere attitudes and emotions.

Knowledge alone — even reading this book — will not bring a rebirth of worship into your life. Worship is not to remain internal and intellectual. That's because worship must be expressed. Yet as I've studied and taught about worship over the past seventeen years, I've discovered that the more I understand, the more I want to worship. It's like watering and caring for a plant so that the flowers can bloom.

My heart's desire is to present great bouquets of worship to my Savior. I invite you to join me. 🌷

PART I

Principles
of
Worship

1

BEING
A
WORSHIPPER

I WANT to tell you something that may surprise you. The Scriptures do not say that God is looking for worship.

> But the hour is coming, and now is, when the true worshipers will worship the Father in spirit and truth; for the Father is seeking such to worship Him (John 4:23).

The Lord is seeking *people who will worship* — not just worship itself. Why? Because He has had worship ever since angels, cherubim and seraphim were created. He does not have a great vacuum inside Himself that can only be filled with worship. He is not insecure. He is self-sufficient and in need of nothing. But He is our Father, and He desires an interactive relationship with His children.

The Greek word that is translated as "seeking" in John 4:23 is *zeteo*. In this context it has the added connotation of "require" or "demand."[1] Our Father is requiring or demanding those who will worship Him in spirit and truth. He seeks after them and pursues them. What does He find when He finds you?

A Lifestyle of Worship

Do you know if you are a worshipper? How can you tell if you are a worshipper in spirit and in truth? Going to church for a few hours a week does not make someone a worshipper. Being a worshipper is more than doing the right things. It is an attitude of life.

Worship is to be continual. It is not to start and stop as songs do, but it is a constant attitude that results in interactive communion with our heavenly Father. David wrote:

> I will bless the Lord at all times; His praise shall continually be in my mouth (Ps. 34:1).

Paul said:

> Therefore by Him let us continually offer the sacrifice of praise to God, that is, the fruit of our lips, giving thanks to His name (Heb. 13:15).

Worshippers spend the entire day with their spirits on the Lord, conscious of giving Him praise.

> My tongue shall speak of Your righteousness
> And of Your praise all the day long (Ps. 35:28).

17

I will extol You, my God, O King;
And I will bless Your name forever and ever.
Every day I will bless You,
And I will praise Your name forever and ever
(Ps. 145:1-2).

Just as you make a habit of reading the Word and praying every day, make a habit of offering up worship every day. This should certainly start in your heart, but let it develop into a "fruit" of your lips as well. Sing a new song to the Lord as you move through the day.

I find it very edifying to my spirit to sing in the car on the way to work or while running errands. Anytime my mind is not concentrating on something, I try to focus it in worship. I'll worship on an airplane or at the mall, walking and talking with the Lord.

Sometimes we make the mistake of thinking that the only time we can worship the Lord is when we are with a group of believers. On the contrary, praise is to be private as well as public. One psalm says: "Let the saints...sing aloud on their beds" (Ps. 149:5). You can worship in your bedroom, in the living room or in your car.

The issue is not where or when but who and how. Any time or place is suitable for worshipping the Father "in spirit and truth" (John 4:23). Jesus said the day will come when we will worship neither in this mountain nor in Jerusalem. Location is an Old Testament, old covenant concept from the time when worship was associated with a tent (the tabernacle of Moses) or a piece of furniture (the ark of the covenant). Paul taught us that we are temples of the Holy Spirit (1 Cor. 6:19; 3:16-17).

Guess what occurs in temples? Worship. We are mobile temples of worship. Wherever we go, worship is appropriate — at the supermarket, the gas station, the office or the mall. A temple of worship is there, so worship is in order.

How do you know you are a worshipper? Worshippers

18

spend time in God's presence. They like to linger there. They are not in a hurry to leave His presence. They worship often because they delight in God's presence and in giving Him honor, reverence and exaltation.

It is their joyous passion. Nothing would frustrate them more than being limited to just a half hour of worship on Sunday mornings.

I believe many Christians are seeing the need, as well as having the desire, to develop a lifestyle of worship. The introduction of worship tapes is in direct response to the desire of believers to worship more than in a church building once a week for an hour or two. With these tapes they are able to sing along and let their spirits commune with the Lord any time and any place.

A Human Desire

Every human being created by God has an innate desire to worship. From the Eskimo Indian to the Aztec Indian, all have worshipped something. We are only satisfied when we come to Christ and learn to be wholehearted worshippers. Then we are fulfilling the purpose for which we were created — to worship Him forever.

Just as you would avoid being a "Sunday morning Christian," don't let yourself become a "Sunday morning worshipper." Let today be the first day of a lifestyle of worship for you.

As you seek to become a worshipper, you may ask yourself, as I did, What *is* worship? Let us look at the foundational principles behind worship. It will help enlighten and expand our understanding of worship. ❧

2

The Living
Heart
of Faith

THE WORSHIP of God is the primary activity of the church and needs no reason beyond itself. According to the Westminster Shorter Catechism, an historic Protestant statement of faith written in 1647, the chief purpose of man is "to glorify God and to enjoy Him forever."[1] Worship is the intended vehicle for inward and total devotion. Worship forms and expresses the believers who participate in it.

Worship has always been seen as the living heart of any religion. The knowledge of worship is essential to the understanding of all religious movements. In these movements worship can be free or formal. Worship involves the expressions and thoughts that come from individuals as a result of an action or activity of God. I believe worship precedes doctrinal formulation, and therefore worship is primary and theology secondary.

Worship is a faithful human response to the revelation of God's being, character, beneficence and will. In worship God is adored simply as who He is. Worship is the requital of God's love in a personal encounter, a communion which is reciprocal but asymmetrical, involving a sacrifice on the part of the created and redeemed. God calls for and enables the renewed response of worship from all believers.

There have been many attempts to define worship. It is a treasure that is hidden in relationship and in the mystery of the Godhead. Defining it is like trying to put a fence around the Great Plains.

How can we define time or the deep love that a man and woman have for each other — not to mention the God-given *agape* love that is at such a higher level? Worship, like love, is hard to define. How can we capture in words the attitude, the passion and the expression of our worship to our champion Savior?

We must be careful that our definitions do not imprison us intellectually or emotionally. Good definitions set boundaries but leave room for enlargement. It is OK to put up walls in an effort to define worship as long as we include a door and some windows. All of our efforts are a mere mortal's attempt at describing our worship relationship with the eternal One.

Good definitions must relate to experience. The Bible does not major in definitions but in descriptions and demonstrations. Unlike a dictionary or encyclopedia, the Bible relates experiences. Therefore, experience is important to definition.

Defining Worship

To make any real progress in our worship journey we must

establish what we mean by *worship. Worship,* in the verb form, means the paying of homage or respect. In the Christian world, the term is used for the reverent devotion, service or honor — whether public or individual — that is paid to God. *Webster's New World Thesaurus* lists the following words as either synonyms or analogous words for worship: adore, admire, celebrate, esteem, exalt, glorify, love, magnify, praise, revere, reverence and venerate.

Worship is the adoration, veneration, exaltation and magnification of God. When we praise, esteem, love, admire and celebrate God, we are worshipping Him. Worship is totally concerned with the *worthiness* of God and not the *worthiness* of the worshipper.

I remember when, as a young teenager, I saw the queen of England for the first time. Her presence caused no small commotion in the frontier logging town of Prince George in the northern part of British Columbia, Canada.

People lined the streets to see Her Majesty Queen Elizabeth and Prince Charles. I was amazed to see almost every segment of society there — waving, bowing and clapping. It didn't matter who they were — drunkards, wild men, the social elite or clergy — they were paying homage to the queen. It was the "worth-ship" of the queen and the throne she sat on that required this worship, not the merit or worth of the worshipper.

Her "worth-ship" had nothing to do with how I felt or if I was in the mood to honor her. We honored her because she was worthy. So it is with the Lord. I do not worship Him because I feel particularly good about myself. I worship Him because of who He is, despite how I feel.

Biblical Definitions

One Hebrew word that is consistently used for worship in the Old Testament is *shahah.* It occurs 172 times. The first time it is mentioned is in Genesis 18:2 where Abraham bowed to the three supernatural visitors, one of which was the Lord.

The translators of the King James Version used five different words or expressions in translating *shabah* — to "prostrate," "bow down," "make obeisance," "do reverence" and "worship." The most frequent translation is "worship." These are mostly action words, requiring body movement. They do not reference a song and only slightly address attitudes. Their focus is on expression through the posture of the body.

Worship is not a sentimental feeling or a flush of emotion. To say "Let us sing one of the songs that Grandpa used to sing" does not necessarily make our adoration more worshipful. Sentiment cannot be called worship. Neither can nostalgia be called worship. Getting a buzz from the music does not make that music worship, though it stirred our emotions. Worship is not something we do to attract unbelievers to our worship service, though that may be a by-product of worship. Worship is *for* the Lord.

Worship is more than a feeling, more than an action and even more than an attitude. It is an attitude expressed. Sometimes the magnitude of the attitude determines the amount of the action. As Bible teacher Judson Cornwall has said, "A lukewarm heart cannot perform boiling hot worship, nor can a rebellious life revere God with any depth of sincerity."

We find in the New Testament three separate Greek words for worship. *Latreuo* possibly means to worship publicly or to render religious service. It is used to describe the service performed by the priests in the temple.

The second word is *sebomai,* meaning to fear or to hold in awe. When we approach the divine presence of the Lord, our reaction or fear gives way at times to reverence and the sense of awe and wonder.

In the New Testament, *proskuneo* is the most commonly used word for worship. This word was a combination of *pros,* meaning "toward," and *kuneo,* meaning "to kiss."[2] Some scholars say that it means to kiss the hand in admiration. Others say it means to kiss the feet in homage. This word is much more descriptive and requires close contact. We can add the kiss of worship to the aspect of bowing in worship. If the Old Testament believers worshipped at a distance in their gestures of worship, New Testament believers are beckoned to come close enough to embrace God, to kiss Him, to touch the Lord in deep-seated worship involving our emotions and our wills.

This aspect of "kissing toward" is more personal and fulfilling. It is the genuineness of worship that is the real issue (John 4:23), not the display or trappings of worship. Worship is a natural outflow of an inward attitude of affection.

Attitude and Action

The words in the Bible that have been translated into worship in English speak of an attitude as being expressed with an action. There is an inference of depth of feeling, closeness and covenant relationship. Worship speaks of communicated affection between man and God. It involves motion, emotion and devotion. It is a release of the deep attitudes of gratitude that are expressed outwardly from the heart of an ardent believer in the presence of a great and holy God.

When you consider all of the words used for worship in both the Old and New Testaments, you find that worship involves both attitudes of awe, reverence and respect as well as actions of bowing, praising and serving. Worship is both a subjective experience and an objective activity. Worship cannot be unexpressed feeling or empty formality. True worship is balanced and involves the mind, the emotions, the will and the body.

If everyone leaves the event of worship with no question as to who is in charge of the universe, the world and every creature therein, if everyone knows who the victorious Lord is, then you've experienced real worship.

When we ask the question of what worship should accomplish, we do not understand what worship is. Those who ask this question are thinking in terms of achieving certain goals. When we approach worship with a goal in mind, we miss its true meaning. The goal-driven approach to worship is ineffective and is not born out of a biblical vision of worship.

In reading Revelation 4 and 5 one does not come away asking: What did worship accomplish here? Heavenly worship represents Jesus Christ. Worship is for Him and to Him. Let us look at a further description of worship.

Praise and Worship

We use the words *praise and worship* to describe actions that arc similar but different. It's important to know the difference between praise and worship because there's an appropriate time for each. At the same time, recognize that everyone does not consider the difference between the terms when they speak, so you often need to listen to the context to understand which concept they're talking about.

Praise is an act of faith. It is extolling the Lord despite how we feel and the circumstances that exist. On the other hand, praise involves sacrifice. Worship does not. We do not worship in faith. We worship out of the attitudes and feelings in our hearts. We love when we worship. We cannot love in faith. We either love the Lord or we do not.

Praise is an instrument of war. It is "high praise" and not "high worship" that executes the judgment written in God's Word (Ps. 149:6-9). Praise is aggressive; worship is submissive and more sensitive. Many churches have highly energetic and aggressive praise services; few ever get to worship ministry.

Praise creates an atmosphere for the presence of the

Lord. Worship is born out of our relationship with God. Praise is what we do as we enter God's presence, and worship is what we do when we get there. We come into His presence singing praises, and, when we find Him, we worship.

Thanksgiving and praise are often based on Christ's deeds, but worship is focused on His Person. We worship because of who He is, not just what He has done for us. Praise and thanksgiving focus more on His acts toward us. One is of a lesser level than the other for this reason. Some know only the acts of God, but few know the ways of God.

Some people may know your acts — the things you have done in your life. However, only your spouse knows your ways, your peculiarities, your uniqueness. How you squeeze the toothpaste. How you sleep. What you like to eat. Likewise, many praise services stay on the level of how the Lord blessed *me* and what He has done for *me,* instead of going beyond that to true love-worship extolling Him for who He is to us.

Let's look at the difference between acts of worship and an attitude of worship. ❦

3

ATTITUDE AND EXPRESSION

WORSHIP IS more an attitude than an outward expression, form or passing emotion. Many times these things get mistaken as worship. Just because people are lifting their hands does not mean they are worshipping.

The outward acts of worship are the least important parts of its expression. They can assist the worshipping heart in expressing its love and adoration, but the acts of worship cannot make a nonworshipping heart into a worshipping one. Worship begins in the heart. The danger is that often acts of worship give a nonworshipping heart the sense of having worshipped.

The critical element is the state of the hearts of the people and not the form of worship. The genesis of worship is the heart of the believer. If it does not begin there, then no matter what the believer does, it is not worship. It may have the look of worship, but it is void of the attitude necessary to be worship.

It is not the performance of the act that makes worship. It is the attitude of love. It is not dancing, bowing or lifting hands that makes worship, but the presence of love. Worship is more an attitude than an action.

Worship Qualities

Worship is recognizing and extolling the Lord's worthiness. It is lauding His attributes and character. It is acclaiming His rank and ability. Worship pays homage to the Lord and gives Him reverence. Worship is not arrogant and flippant. Believers who hold those attitudes when they claim to worship are not worshippers. Worship comes from a broken spirit and a contrite heart.

Worship involves prayer. Prayer births and matures a relationship with the Lord, and out of that relationship we worship the Lord. Worship acts without prayer could be mere performances that smell of earthly flesh and not the heavenly fragrance of something meant for the Lord.

Worship is expressing admiration to the One we adore. Worship is an attitude that recognizes the superiority of Christ and acknowledges our dependence on Him.

Worship is an attitude that requires the right words. In worship we choose our words carefully because they communicate the key ingredient and the motivation of our worship — our heart attitudes. The words cannot be shallow and irrelevant. They have to say what we are feeling in a way that is just right. It sometimes seems so vain to try to communicate the thoughts we have for our exalted Lord when we know He sees our hearts anyway and knows our thoughts before we think them.

Honesty, reverence and devotion require the correct words. They require fresh words and fresh thoughts. Yesterday's songs of worship are old and stale, like bread left out overnight. Words that are hot out of the oven of our hearts are much more appropriate in worship. They must be our own words — not just someone else's words. We must mean them, and they must be "us." They are words that communicate our hearts correctly.

Worship is varied expressions of different individuals loving and reverencing God all at the same time. Therefore, each one can express worship in his or her own manner. Sameness is not our goal in worship services. We are to be ourselves and communicate our own individual expressions of worship. Our methods of expressing love and adoration differ, and those differences will lend flavor and color to the worship when homogenized together.

We are not to copy one another and call it "our" worship. And we are not to let someone else do the worship for us. The pastor or worship leader cannot be a surrogate for our own worship. One cannot do it for everyone. Worship requires each one to express his own attitudes to the Lord. My attitudes will not work for your attitudes and vice versa.

What a person worships is a good indication of what is really valuable to him. We worship that which is worthy in our eyes. In Malaysia, many Chinese people worship their deceased relatives because they regard them highly. In Japan, people worship the idol Buddha because of their belief in Buddhism.

True worship should lead to personal enrichment and enablement, the kind of spiritual strength that helps believers carry the burdens and fight the battles of life. True worship brings a revelation or awareness of the Lord. In that experience are a refreshing and an empowerment that come from His presence. Worship rejuvenates the believer.

Those who feel tired, thirsty, hungry and weak during worship may not have worshipped at all because they are still self-conscious and not God-conscious. How can one worship the Lord with all that is within him — in honesty and genuineness — and be thinking, When will this be over? I'm hungry.

How can we change from being self-conscious to being God-conscious? I believe the first step is recognizing that we are called to worship. It's not just an *extra* thing we can do. It's essential to being a Christian.

4

CALLED
TO
WORSHIP

WHEN I was a child growing up in the church, I was taught that the most important part of being a Christian was to be a witness. As a teenager, I was told again that the single calling in my life was to be a soul-winner.

Evangelism is a very important part of the mission of the church, but it is not the most important. Worship is. The church is first a worshipping community before it is anything else.

Worship is the "work of the people" in the sense that it calls for active participation of the whole assembly. Each member has a role. It is the believer's utmost priority and highest occupation.

The Lord Himself Calls Us to Worship Him

Worship is the first commandment God gave to Moses for the people of Israel.

> And God spoke all these words, saying:
> I am the Lord your God, who brought you out
> of the land of Egypt, out of the house of
> bondage.
> You shall have no other gods before Me (Ex. 20:1-3).

God's second commandment dealt with worship too.

> You shall have no other gods before or besides
> Me. You shall not make yourself any graven
> image (to worship it)...You shall not bow
> down yourself to them or serve them; for I
> the Lord your God am a jealous God (Ex.
> 20:3-5, AMP).

Not only does God claim the first place, but He reveals His intolerance of everything that would deprive Him of the highest position. Many things in our lives attempt to draw our hearts away from God as the supreme object of our affection. The apostle John warned:

> Little children, keep yourselves from idols (1
> John 5:21).

It is dreadfully possible for self, in its many and varied forms, to ascend the throne of the heart and displace God in the believer's life, so that little or no worship ascends to Him. Other things or people that we honor before Him can also be idols. They redirect affection that was meant for the Lord.

"Can a man rob God?" (Mal. 3:8). The Lord Himself posed this question, referring to those who were holding back their tithes. In the same way, many believers, for one cause or another, are withholding from God the worship He seeks and has every right to expect. We withhold whole-hearted, selfless worship for many reasons. We explain that we don't believe in certain expressions or we have already spent too much time worshipping. In either case, we only think of ourselves and don't give the Lord what He wants.

Jesus showed the primary importance that worship should have in prayer. "When you pray, say, [Our] Father, [Who is in heaven] hallowed be Your name" (Luke 11:2, AMP). When we pray, worship is the first order of business. Exaltation of Him is primary. Then we can make petitions.

Eternity Calls Us to Worship

The worship which begins on earth is but the prelude to our eternal occupation. We were saved to worship our heavenly Father forever.

Before the Lord gave the apostle John his marvelous vision of things to come, He impressed upon John's heart the vital place and the vast importance that worship has in eternity.

John, the worshipper of Jesus, saw before him a throne in heaven. The twenty-four elders who sat before the throne and the four living creatures continually cried out: "Holy, holy, holy, Lord God Almighty, who was, and is and is to come!" (Rev. 4:8). As these living creatures gave glory and honor to Him who sits upon the throne, the twenty-four elders fell down before God and worshipped Him, saying:

> Worthy are You, our Lord and God, to receive the glory and the honor and dominion, for You created all things; by Your will they were [brought into being] and were created (Rev. 4:11, AMP).

In Revelation 5, Jesus, the Lion of the tribe of Judah, the root of David, the only one worthy and able to open the seals of the book, came forward. The elders of heaven and the four living creatures fell down prostrate before the Lamb, and they sang a magnificent new hymn of worship:

> You are worthy to take the scroll and to break the seals that are on it, for You were slain (sacrificed) and with Your blood You purchased men unto God from every tribe and language and people and nation. And You have made them a kingdom [royal race] and priests to our God, and they shall reign [as kings] over the earth! (Rev. 5:9-10, AMP).

Then, around the throne, the voices of myriads of angels took up the refrain and sang:

> Worthy is the Lamb who was slain to receive power and riches and wisdom, and strength and honor and glory and blessing! (Rev. 5:12).

Following the song of the angels, John heard the united voice of every creature in heaven, on the earth, under the earth and in the sea, saying in harmonious accord:

> Blessing and honor and glory, and power be to Him who sits on the throne, and to the Lamb, forever and ever! (Rev. 5:13).

At this, the four living creatures before the throne responded "Amen," and the twenty-four elders "fell down and worshiped Him who lives forever and ever" (Rev. 5:14).

What a glorious day when all the redeemed of all the ages and of all races will be gathered together in the presence of the One whose precious blood has brought them there! The vast volume of this eternal worship service will be rich with majestic harmony and exquisite cadence, all declaring the intrinsic worthiness of the eternal Godhead.

The Scriptures Call Us to Worship

The Bible contains hundreds of different reasons to praise the Lord. No other writer expressed this passion for worshipping the Lord more eloquently than King David.

Give thanks to the Lord, call on his name;
make known among the nations what he has done.
Sing to him, sing praise to him;
tell of all his wonderful acts.
Glory in his holy name;
let the hearts of those who seek the Lord rejoice (1 Chron. 16:8-10, NIV).

Ascribe to the Lord, O families of nations,
ascribe to the Lord glory and strength,
ascribe to the Lord the glory due his name.
Bring an offering and come before him;
worship the Lord in the splendor of his holiness (1 Chron. 16:28-29, NIV).

David wrote this song of thanksgiving after he brought the ark of the covenant back to Jerusalem. As you read the Bible, notice the exhortations to worship and their context. It will bring tremendous understanding in how worship can be a practical part of our lives.

Worship Is in Man's Nature

Every civilization and culture in world history have worshipped something or somebody. Every pagan, every primitive savage, every materialist, every atheist and every agnostic have some material god of their own invention.

Why? Because man was created to worship. We were manufactured, constructed and equipped to reverence and pay homage to the One who shaped us. It is in our makeup to give exaltation to one who is superior to us. It is man's nature to praise and worship God the Creator.

> The people whom I formed for Myself
> Will declare My praise (Is. 43:21).

God has exclusive rights to our adoration because He made us and equipped us to praise Him. A. W. Tozer recognized this when he wrote:

> The purpose of God in sending His Son to die and live and be at the right hand of God the Father was that He might restore to us the missing jewel, the jewel of worship; that we might come back and learn to do again that which we were created to do in the first place — worship the Lord in the beauty of holiness, to spend our lives in awesome wonder and adoration of God.[1]

Worship is our most important and meaningful occupation in life. John MacArthur, pastor of Grace Community Church in Sun Valley, California, has stated that worship is not an addendum to life; it is at life's core.

Man is at his best when he is praising God. There is nothing a child of God can do in life that is more appropriate or beneficial than to worship the Lord. There is never a time when worship or praise is improper.

> Praise is becoming to the upright (Ps. 33:1, NAS).

The Hebrew word for *becoming* is *navah,* which could also be translated as "fitting" or "seemly."[2] It is fitting, suitable, correct and appropriate for us to worship. Worship looks good on us.

The Holy Spirit Calls Us to Worship Him

Paul exhorted the Ephesians:

> Be filled and stimulated with the (Holy) Spirit (Eph. 5:18, AMP).

What happens when we are filled and stimulated with the Holy Spirit? Verse 19 tells us:

> Speak out to one another in psalms and hymns and spiritual songs, offering praise with voices [and instruments], and making melody with all your heart to the Lord (AMP).

Paul also wrote, "I will sing with my spirit" (1 Cor. 14:15). How can I sing with "my spirit"? It is through the power of the Holy Spirit. Paul explained this by saying, "If I pray in a tongue, my spirit prays" (1 Cor. 14:14). In other words, the Holy Spirit (who administers the gift of tongues) is the One who gives us the words to express what is in our spirits. That expression may come in prayers or in the singing of "Spirit" songs.

One of the chief functions of the office of the Holy Spirit is to exalt the Lamb of God, the Lord Jesus Christ. That is the essence of worship. John 15:26 states:

> When the Comforter is come,...even the Spirit of truth, which proceedeth from the Father, he shall testify of me (KJV).

When we are full of the Holy Spirit, we will bless the Lord. That is the work of the Spirit of God.

> Zacharias was filled with the Holy Spirit, and prophesied, saying: "Blessed be the Lord God of Israel" (Luke 1:67).

The Holy Spirit is intrinsically involved in exalting the Lord Most High. He not only calls us to worship but enables us to worship. The Holy Spirit gives us the music of worship, the lyrics of worship and the desire to worship. He is the unction within us that causes our worship to bubble up out of our bellies. Jesus said:

> He who believes in Me, as the Scripture said, "From his innermost being shall flow rivers of living water" (John 7:38, NAS).

The apostle John explained:

> This He spoke of the Spirit, whom those who believed in Him were to receive (John 7:39, NAS).

So the Holy Spirit is like a spring, filling us with living worship that will flow forth from our spirits like a river.

Our Salvation Calls Us to Worship Him

The songs coming from those for whom Christ died are very special. Believers are the only source of the songs of redemption. Without us, the worship of all creation is not complete.

The Lord saved us in order to restore fellowship with Him, and that includes worship. Those who receive so great a salvation respond naturally with gratitude and praise. No other power can do what our Savior did. It merits an everlasting ovation of worship.

Believers render worship on behalf of a world which is not yet able or willing to worship. God's primary purpose for our salvation is not to make us witnesses but to make us worshippers. The Lord wants to reveal to us His presence in the midst of our worship. Then others, too, would make Him their Lord.

Church Leaders Call Us to Worship

Many great Christian leaders over the last fifty years have spoken of a churchwide rebirth of worship. Devotional writer and preacher A. W. Tozer spoke eloquently of it:

> We're organized, we work, we have our agencies. We have almost everything, but there's one thing that the churches, even the gospel churches, do not have: that is the ability to worship. We are not cultivating the art of worship. It's the one shining gem that is lost to the modern church, and I believe that we ought to search for this until we find it.[3]

Charles Stanley, pastor of the First Baptist Church of Atlanta, Georgia, saw the beginnings of change a few years ago.

> Something is happening in our form of worship. That is, something that has been missing a very long time is beginning to make its way into worship services all over this world. There has been, for too long, an absence of genuine, true praise to Almighty God...The Holy Spirit is invading this generation and enabling the church of the Lord Jesus Christ to fulfill its goal to exalt and praise Almighty God.[4]

Jack Hayford, senior pastor of the Church on the Way in Van Nuys, California, has become a leader in the modern call for worship. He wrote:

> God has given us much work to do as a people. Therefore, our foremost task is to become a people of much worship. We must precede all, and all must proceed with worship.[5]

Churches all over the world and across denominations are experiencing a rebirth of worship in their services. Of course, this rebirth comes about only as individuals such as you and I respond to the urging of the Holy Spirit in our hearts.

All Creation Calls Us to Worship Him

The Bible speaks often of creation worshipping the Creator.

All Your works shall praise You, O Lord, and Your loving ones shall bless You — affectionately and gratefully shall Your saints confess and praise You (Ps. 145:10, AMP).

And again in Psalm 69:34:

Let heaven and earth praise Him,
The seas and everything that moves in them.

All creation worships the Creator. There is not anything made that does not reverence, think highly or greatly appreciate the One who created it. The Scriptures are clear on how much all the works of God praise Him.

Let the field be exultant, and all that is in it! Then shall all the trees of the wood sing for joy (Ps. 96:12, AMP).

Not only does the vegetable world praise the Lord, but the land itself also rejoices in its Creator.

The Lord reigns; let the earth rejoice; let the multitude of isles and coastlands be glad! (Ps. 97:1, AMP).

Vegetables, animals and land even join together to offer concerts of praise.

The luxuriant pastures in the uncultivated country drip (with moisture), and the hills gird themselves with joy. The meadows are clothed with flocks, the valleys also are covered with grain, they shout for joy and sing together (Ps. 65:12-13, AMP).

When the psalmist's heart was overflowing with worship, the Holy Spirit within him cried out to creation to join in praise.

Praise Him, all His angels, praise Him, all His host! Praise Him, sun and moon, praise Him, all you stars of light! Praise Him, you highest heavens, and you waters above the heavens! Let them praise the name of the Lord, for He commanded, and they were created. Praise the Lord from the earth, you sea monsters and all deeps, you lightning, hail, fog and frost, you stormy wind fulfilling His orders! Mountains and all hills, fruitful trees and all cedars, beasts and all cattle, creeping things and flying birds! (Ps. 148:2-5,7-10, AMP).

Doesn't your spirit soar as you read these words?

Sing, O heavens, for the Lord has done it; shout, you depths of the earth; break forth into singing, you mountains, O forest, and every tree in it! For the Lord has redeemed Jacob, and will glorify Himself in Israel (Is. 44:23, AMP).

And again in Isaiah 49:13:

Sing for joy, O heavens, and be joyful, O earth, and break forth into singing, O mountains; for the Lord has comforted His people and will have compassion upon His afflicted (AMP).

As the prophet Habakkuk said:

> His glory covered the heavens,
> And the earth was full of His praise (Hab. 3:3).

There was a time when praise filled the earth, and there will be a time again as all creation and regenerated man worship the Lord.

> And every creature which is in heaven and on the earth and under the earth and such as are in the sea, and all that are in them, I heard saying:
>
> "Blessing and honor and glory and power,
> Be to Him who sits on the throne,
> And to the Lamb, forever and ever!" (Rev. 5:13).

Angels, Seraphim and Cherubim
Call Us to Worship Him

When the seraphim cry out in worship, it is an incitement to humanity to worship. John described the scene of worship in the throne room of God.

> Whenever the living creatures give glory and honor and thanks to Him who sits on the throne, who lives forever and ever, the twenty-four elders fall down before Him who sits on the throne and worship Him (Rev. 4:9-10).

The leadership in heaven responded to the worship of the living creatures. They *fell* down. They did not *lie* down and worship Him. They were so overwhelmed by the presence of God in His majesty that they just could not stand up anymore.

The Scriptures say that angelic beings are worshipping the Lord continually.

In the midst of the throne, and around the throne, were four living creatures...They do not rest day or night, saying:

Holy, holy, holy,
Lord God Almighty,
Who was and is and is to come! (Rev. 4:6-8).

He Calls; We Choose

Most of creation worships instinctively. But God made man in His image with the ability to create, imagine, dream and make decisions. So we have the ability to decide whether we want to worship the Lord our Creator or not.

We can give to God our Father, to whom we owe everything, that which will bring delight to His heart! How tragic it is to think that so many Christians, either through ignorance of or disobedience to this revelation, are keeping from their heavenly Father that which He so ardently desires them to give Him!

This is something that nothing else in creation can give Him as we can. Angels cannot sing the songs of redemption, nor can mountains or animals — though these do praise their Creator. It is only man who has the option of choice.

The call is clear. ❦

5

WORSHIP DOESN'T
END WITH
THE SONG SERVICE

WHEN YOU hear the word *worship,* what is the first image that comes to your mind? For many people it is their song service at church. They perceive the worship time as when they sing slower, more intimate songs.

This misconception is implied unknowingly within Pentecostal and charismatic groups. But a worship service is just what the name says — worship the whole way through. There's worship in all parts of a worship service: prayers, music, creeds, Scripture reading, silences, offerings, sermons and celebration of the Lord's supper.

The practice of worship is directly related to what we

believe worship to be. If a church believes worship to be singing, then all its energy will be focused on that aspect of the service, and the congregation will squirm and fidget if the sermon "drags" on too long. The problem with basing worship on just one definition is that you're limited to only one aspect of the truth.

Let's look at how all the functions of a worship service draw our hearts toward the presence of the Lord.

Prayers

Prayer is a worship function that requires the right words. We choose our words carefully because they communicate the key ingredient and the motivation of our worship — our heart attitude. The words cannot be shallow or irrelevant. We must mean them, and they must be "us."

Is it right to adopt the words of a prayer from a prayer book? Can we compose our prayers ahead of time and offer them to God later? Are they better if we just make them up on the spot?

I believe the answer lies in the heart. Remember that worship is an attitude and an expression. If you find or prepare a prayer that reflects your attitude, then its sincere expression is worship. The church has historically used prayers of affirmation and thanksgiving, repentance, dedication and illumination in worship.

On the other hand, if a prepared prayer does not express what's in your heart, then reading it out loud is in no way worship. And just because a prayer is unrehearsed does not make it any more sincere. The attitude of the heart is the deciding factor.

When we pray in a heavenly language, we communicate directly to the Lord. Yet we still need the attitude of our hearts to be that of worship to the Lord. If the attitude is not focused on the Lord, then worship may not occur. Just because someone uses a heavenly language, especially in a joking manner, I do not believe worship occurs at that moment.

Music

I love music, but I have come to the conclusion that there is no such thing as "worship music." Worship is in the person — not the music.

While music itself is not worship, it can express one's attitudes of worship. Deep, emotional feelings are sometimes better expressed through song than through spoken words. Music gives vocabulary to worship as well as unites worshippers, helping them to focus on a certain aspect of the Lord.

I have found over two hundred Scripture verses that tell us to sing praises to the Lord.[1]

Sing praises to God, sing praises! Sing praises to our King, sing praises! (Ps. 47:6).

Come before His presence with singing (Ps. 100:2).

Musical instruments are also referred to many times in Scripture. We are *commanded* to play musical instruments to the Lord in worship.

Praise Him with trumpet sound; praise Him with lute and harp! Praise Him with tambourine and (single or group) dance; praise Him with stringed and wind instruments or flutes! Praise Him with sounding cymbals; praise Him with loud clashing cymbals (Ps. 150:3-5, AMP).

The tricky thing about music is that we can play songs with worshipful words and we may still not be worshipping. It could be sounding brass and tinkling cymbals because there is no love in the song. It's an attitude from the heart that turns music into worship.

Only the Lord sees hearts; yet we can discern whether those who have the posture and sound of worship are attempting to worship. Usually other things will give them away; for example, where they are looking while they are singing. I have seen some worship teams sing lyrics to the Lord and at the same time look at the congregation as if they are the audience.

In worship, the Lord is the audience. In music, people are the audience. There is a *big* difference. Our actions must be consistent with our heart attitude in worship.

Raising Hands

One of the most wonderful expressions of Pentecostal/charismatic worship is raising hands. It is a physical expression that is symbolic of our inner desires to reach out to God.

> Let us lift our hearts and hands to God in heaven (Lam. 3:41).

> I desire therefore that the men pray everywhere, lifting up holy hands (1 Tim. 2:8).

The Scriptures encourage many physical acts of worship. We are exhorted not only to kneel before the Lord but to dance, bow, lie prostrate, clap and shout in our worship (Ps. 150:4; 95:6).

Creeds and Readings

Creeds are not often used in charismatic churches, though a growing minority is recognizing them. The value of creeds, such as the Apostles', the Athanasian and the Nicene, is that they remind us what we believe and provide a link of worship to the past. It's too easy to cut all ties with the history of the church when we leave the old to "go on to perfection" (Heb. 6:1). Yet all that we are and believe comes from the revelation the Lord has given in the past.

Some charismatics have the impression that only dead churches have readings. There are not really as many dead readings as there are dead readers. If a reading expresses what is in a worshipper's heart, then it can be a powerful vehicle of worship. If the reading is not what's in the heart, then the worshipper should speak to the Lord in his or her own words as well.

A worship leader can begin a service with everyone following him in reciting a creed. This will focus everyone and be a powerful tool of proclamation, serving notice to the kingdom of darkness that the church is alive and unified.

In our devotional lives we can read or declare a creed as we prepare our hearts to worship.

Many early church fathers in the third century were scarred and maimed by the persecution they suffered in declaring their belief in the trinity and in Christ's claim of deity. During the Arian controversy, 318 church fathers met at Nicaea and adopted a statement of faith called the Nicene Creed. For more than sixteen hundred years it has stood as the final test of orthodoxy. This ancient creed has been held by Eastern and Western branches of the church and by all but a small minority of Christians.[2]

The Nicene Creed and others have been forged out by great Christian minds and have stood the test of almost two millennia. Declaring these creeds brings an historical aspect to our charismatic worship. It ties us into worship that believers have been declaring for hundreds of years. Creeds such as the Nicene reveal a rebirth of worship in those who wrote them and in the believers who declared them. We should reconsider this form of worship renewal that has empowered so many believers!

The
Nicene Creed

I believe in one God the Father Almighty, Maker of heaven and earth, and of all things visible and invisible:

And in one Lord Jesus Christ, the only begotten Son of God, begotten of His Father before all worlds, God of God, Light of Light, very God of very God, begotten, not made, being of one substance with the Father, by whom all things were made;

Who for us men and for our salvation came down from heaven, and was incarnate by the Holy Spirit, of the Virgin Mary, and was made man, and crucified also for us under Pontius Pilate; He suffered and was buried, and the third day He rose again according to the Scriptures, and ascended into heaven, and sitteth on the right hand of the Father;

And He shall come again with glory to judge both the quick and the dead;

Whose kingdom shall have no end.

And I believe in the Holy Spirit, the Lord and Giver of life, who proceedeth from the Father and the Son, who with the Father and the Son together is worshiped and glorified; who spoke by the prophets. And I believe in one catholic and apostolic church; I acknowledge one baptism for the remission of sins, and I look for the resurrection of the dead, and the life of the world to come.

Amen.

Silences

During worship services in the Mennonite church in which I grew up, we would sometimes observe times of silence. Some people may look at those times of seeming inactivity as a sign of deadness. However, those were times when believers were still and quiet so that they could think about their God. Times of silence may be necessary for two reasons: 1) to dig up from the depths of our soul those things that need to be given to the Lord and 2) to let God do the digging and pointing and speak to us.

If we do all the vocalizing in a worship service, when does God speak except in prophecy and preaching? If we are silent He can then speak to us individually; that action of God in our lives will inspire further worship.

Offerings

I have really enjoyed a trend I've seen in several churches recently. When the offering is announced, the congregation breaks into applause, symbolizing their joy in worshipping the Lord through giving.

Even if your church doesn't clap for offerings, as you give your gifts to the Lord, remember that you are performing an act of worship.

I am learning that I must be more and more selfless. Worshippers are trying constantly to dethrone self. In giving offerings we are giving away something that self wants to keep. Offerings keep our hearts postured correctly.

Sermons

Preaching as an act of worship? It seems so obvious, but do we live out this concept in our worship services?

Preaching as worship starts with the preacher. The outline of a sermon is not a message from God any more than a recipe is a meal or a blueprint is a building. But when the preacher speaks with an attitude of bringing glory to God, then the delivery of the message is an act of worship in itself.

When preaching is an act of worship, it won't just reveal facts about God — it will reveal God Himself. Do you listen for a revelation of God during the sermon, or are you just listening for information or waiting to go home? The preacher is leading worship. Are you following?

Let your heart be stirred by the vision of God, and the Spirit of God will say far more to you than what the minister declares from the pulpit. The sermon becomes like a prism from a shaft of sunlight; it highlights a portion of divine thought so that its beauty and wonder are clearly seen. Instead of just listening, we are worshipping.

If preaching is an act of worship, there is an immediacy to the impact of the Word. I have wondered if it is wise for people to take detailed notes during the sermon. How can the Word impact you and bring you to worship if you are busy writing? If your attention is on the preacher, the delivery, the text, the content, the structure of the sermon — then the sermon is not a worship experience. For some, however, it may be possible to worship while they are taking notes and the Lord is speaking to them.

As Martin Luther reportedly said, "When thou hearest the Word of God with all thy heart, thou dost offer sacrifice." Great heights of adoration, praise and worship can be reached by a devout congregation as the things of God pass before them during the sermon.

The Lord's Supper

The Lord's supper, or Eucharist, as it was called among Christians since the second century, has been the heart of Christian worship throughout church history. It comes from the last supper of Jesus with His disciples before His crucifixion. The word *Eucharist* means "thanksgiving." It refers to the prayer-pattern used by Jews before eating in which they blessed and thanked God for what He had done for His people.

The Lord's supper is one of the most meaningful and celebratory moments in worship — never to be a sad time or a long introspective time. It focuses on remembering what Jesus has done for us, not searching for hidden sin, although that has a part to play in the Lord's supper as we examine ourselves. The focus must be on Jesus for the Lord's supper to be worship. Families can take the Lord's supper at home during family devotions or at the reuniting of relatives.

No Preliminaries

If our worship has good theology and our theology has good worship, from the beginning of the service to the end it is a worship experience. There are no preliminaries to get out of the way; there is no boring sermon to sit through. We gather to encounter the Lord from the first prayer to the final invocation.

Furthermore, these things aren't worship just because a group of believers is doing them together. True, the Lord comes when two or three are gathered in prayer, but He is filled with joy when you pray alone too. God is just as thrilled by your song of praise in the car as He is by the worship of a hundred voices. You're even worshipping when you write a check to give to the work of the Lord! A rebirth of worship in church can carry over into all of life if the attitude of the expression is focused on the Lord. All we do in word and deed we do as unto the Lord. ❦

WHOLEHEARTED WORSHIP

WHEN I fell in love with my wife, I spent every moment of the day thinking about and planning for her. When we were together, it seemed as if we were the only two people on earth.

I wasn't savvy enough to give away part of my heart and keep part for myself. I gave it all to her. She had my focus, my attention, my heart. We hugged and held hands as often as we could. We spent as much time as we could together. Our expressions of affection were not mechanical or dutiful but packed with feeling and meaning. We were focused intensely on each other.

Jesus described this kind of love when the scribe asked

Him, "What is the foremost commandment?"

Jesus answered with a question: "What does the law say?"

The lawyer replied:

You shall love the Lord your God with all your heart, and with all your soul, and with all your mind, and with all your strength (Mark 12:30).

Jesus told the lawyer he was correct.

That's all-ways kind of love. It is not long, ongoing love, but all-total-complete love. It's the first commandment of the old covenant and the greatest commandment of the new covenant. Let's look at the four ways we can show the Lord our love.

With All Your Heart

I cannot sing songs of worship or express actions of worship if they do not come from my heart. I cannot mimic somebody else and call it worship. It must be "me." It must have a part of me in it — a piece of my heart, affection, reverence and so on.

Sometimes worship leaders will suggest different expressions of worship for their congregations, such as standing up or raising hands. Following their instructions can bring you into wholehearted worship. But simply following instructions is not worship.

Nor can someone on the platform be a substitute for you. We must express our own worship from our own hearts.

When you are a wholehearted worshipper, you will never get to the point where you say, "God, I gave You enough. The rest I will keep for myself." You'll want to give Him everything. Wholehearted worshippers are unreasonable in their lavish veneration. They are excessive and extravagant. It is hard for a stingy person to worship biblically. Biblical worshippers are generous because they are wholehearted worshippers.

Whole-Soul Worship

"Wow! What a show!"

"Did you see that play?"

"What a home run!"

To jump for joy at a sports event is not unusual. Then why do some consider it wrong to jump for joy because of the Christ event — the greatest "grand slam" and "touchdown" in all of history? A sports event does not change our lives, our beings and our worship. The Christ event does all of that and much more. It calls for a celebration with greater emotion than any show, speech or game. It's a celebration for "all your soul" (Mark 12:30).

How do we love the Lord with all our souls? One aspect of our souls is our emotions. Therefore, to love the Lord with all your soul includes your emotions.

Though our worship is not based on feelings, we can be emotional when we worship the Lord. The Lord delights in worship that is with *all* our emotions. It is not sacrilegious or irreverent to express emotion in worship.

I remember standing on the platform in the Muslim country of Malaysia and seeing four thousand Chinese, East Indian and Malaysian Christians singing, clapping and dancing with all of their might. This kind of emotional exuberance was not typical of those cultures. Why were they so wholehearted? They were doing something they were created to do — worship their Creator and make His praise as great as He is (Ps. 48:10).

I saw the same thing in Costa Rica — believers abandoned to loud, intense praise to the King of all nations. I stood in the midst of that group and cried. The emotion and fervor of those saints warmed my heart, convicted me of lukewarmness and made me hungry for what they had. Sincere, wholehearted worship will do that — make others hungry to worship the Lord themselves.

The Scriptures teem with examples of emotional worship.

> Cry out and shout, O inhabitant of Zion,
> For great is the Holy One of Israel in your
>   midst! (Is. 12:6).

> Sing, O barren,
> You who have not borne!
> Break forth into singing, and cry aloud (Is.
>   54:1).

> Bless — affectionately, gratefully praise — the Lord, O my soul, and all that is (deepest) within me, bless His holy name... (Ps. 103:1, AMP).

God made us to express extreme emotion. It is a normal human response to the things that we encounter in our lives. Worshippers are free to experience and express what they feel. Some of us need this freedom to bring wholeness to our emotional lives.

Since true worship is the response of a whole person to God, then removing emotions from our Christian worship is unnatural and ungodly. Unemotional worship is man-made, man-ordained, religious paraphernalia.

Some churches are proud that their doctrine is correct. They never have emotional excesses or get "carried away." But they don't realize that they've corrected the life and the spirit out of their worship. They're neither hot nor cold but disgustingly lukewarm (Rev. 3:16). Our worship should not only be internalized and intellectualized but experiential and expressive.

Noisy Worship

> Make them joyful in my house of *prayer* (Is. 56:7,
> italics added).

The word *prayer*, or *tephillah* is used in Psalms to refer to a "prayer set to music and sung in the formal worship service."[1] These oral expressions to God, mixed with joy, are noisy and are to be in the house of prayer. God made them joyful. Joy is an emotion that is often expressed audibly.

The Lord's house is to be a place of noise, a place of joyous celebration. It is a medieval notion that we are to be silent and stoic in our public Christian worship.

The very use of the word *hallelujah* in the liturgy of the Scriptures suggests the aspect of excited worship. The word *hallelujah* is a spontaneous outcry of one excited about God. It is a combination of two Hebrew words: *halal* and *yah*. *Halal* means "to boast, to shout praise."[2] *Yah* appears to be a contracted form of YHWH, the unspoken Hebrew name for God in the Old Testament. Literally, then, *hallelujah* means "praise God." The word was used to express extreme excitement, exuberance and exultation.

> After this I heard what sounded like a mighty
> shout of a great crowd in heaven, exclaiming,
> Hallelujah — praise the Lord! Salvation and glory
> (splendor and majesty) and power (dominion
> and authority [belong]) to our God!...And again
> they shouted, Hallelujah — praise the Lord! (Rev.
> 19:1,3, AMP).

This is the natural behavior of all believers in the presence of our Lord.

Mutual Pleasure

One of the strongest emotions of worship is pleasure.

Worship is entirely for the pleasure of our Creator.

> Let Israel be glad in his Maker;
> Let the sons of Zion rejoice in their King.
> Let them praise His name with dancing;
> Let them sing praises to Him with timbrel and
> lyre.
> For the Lord takes pleasure in His people (Ps.
> 149:2-4, NAS).

Yet we discover that worship brings us great pleasure as well. As Graham Kendrick said:

> Worship is first and foremost for His benefit, not ours, though it is marvelous to discover that in giving Him pleasure, we ourselves enter into what can become our richest and most wholesome experience in life.[3]

Though we often "feel good" when we worship, we do not base our worship on emotions. We worship because Jesus died, was buried, rose from the grave, ascended on high, sat down at the right hand of the Father and is coming again.

Whole-Mind Worship

Whole-mind worship has two facets: focus and intelligence.

First, worshipping with all of your mind means focusing intensely on the object of worship. You cannot be easily distracted when engaged in this intense exaltation. You are God-conscious. When you worship with all of your mind, you won't be thinking, Will this be over soon? I wonder what restaurants are open after the service.

Second, whole-mind worship is also intelligent worship.

Sometimes our charismatic or Pentecostal worship comes mainly from the soul or feeling realm, and the theology of God is lacking. To worship God because of His attributes and character, we need to comprehend a revelation of Him with our intellect. Meditating on the Word and the character of God will spark spirited worship.

Perhaps we should have more times of reflection on the Lord during worship services. Our worship does not need to be loud to be true worship. Meditating on the Lord is appropriate before, during and after worship.

Without reflection or meditation, we often do not have proper motivation for our worship. Our desire to worship the Lord should come from the impression He makes on us.

Whole-Strength Worship

Our bodies are our source of physical strength, and they were created for expressing worship to the Lord. They are to be dedicated to God as living sacrifices for ministry and worship.

> I appeal to you therefore, brethren, and beg of you in view of [all] the mercies of God, to make a decisive dedication of your bodies — presenting all your members and faculties — as a living sacrifice, holy (devoted, consecrated) and well-pleasing to God, which is your reasonable (rational, intelligent) service and spiritual worship (Rom. 12:1, AMP).

Notice that God is "well-pleased" by whole-body sacrifices.

Our bodies are temples, worship sanctuaries, of the Holy Spirit who lives in us (1 Cor. 6:19). We are not our own. Christ bought our bodies with His life.

Do you not know that your body is a temple of the Holy Spirit, who is in you, whom you have from God, and that you are not your own? For you have been bought with a price: therefore glorify God in your body (1 Cor. 6:20).

We are to worship God both *in* our bodies and *with* our bodies.

We were created to fulfill the greatest commandment — loving the Lord our God with all our hearts, minds, souls and strength. I love the way Don McMinn, minister of praise and worship at First Southern Baptist Church of Del City, Oklahoma, explains it:

Our entire being is fashioned as an instrument of praise. Just as a master violin maker designs an instrument to produce maximum aesthetic results, so God tailor-made our bodies, souls and spirits to work together in consonance to produce pleasing expressions of praise and worship. When we use body language to express praise, that which is internal becomes visible.[4]

The Scriptures say:

Give unto the Lord, O you mighty ones,
Give unto the Lord glory and strength (Ps. 29:1).

How do we give unto the Lord our strength if our bodies are not involved?

Words With Heart

Worship is to be wholehearted, passion-pregnant and meaningful. If it doesn't touch our souls, our hearts, our strength and our minds, then it is not as meaningful.

Worship is personal and passionate. When I worship, I would rather my heart be without words than my words without heart.

Having this kind of wholeheartedness in our worship results naturally in expressing ourselves in movement. It is a logical next step for the biblical worshipper. Let's see why we as believers need not be ashamed of devotion in motion. ❦

7

WORSHIP HIM
WITH
THE DANCE

A SOCCER player jumps when he scores a much-needed goal. A college student who is nervous about her test results dances around the dorm when she hears she passed with good grades. When your neighbor finds out he has won a million dollars in a maga-zine sweepstakes, he may leap in the air. Why? Expressive movement is something that is natural to us.

Yet in our Western culture we discourage people from acting natural in Christian worship. If Christ has changed your life, then you have every reason to wave your arms, jump up and down or dance for sheer joy.

I have ministered in two Southern Baptist churches in

which the entire congregation danced in the worship service. In one of them the whole youth group came to the front during the worship service and danced during every song. When it was time to pray, all the men came forward and knelt in prayer. What great expressions of worship!

During the 1970s and 1980s, some churches experienced phenomenal growth. People were attracted to church bodies where they could worship freely according to biblical patterns. Those who knew a freedom in their spirits wanted to have the freedom to express it through worship.

To have a renewed life of worship and then to restrict your body from expressing that renewed heart would be to hide and eventually kill the new life of worship that God had given you.

An Act of the Will

Some have described "dancing in the Spirit" as a high spiritual state. However, this is not a biblical concept. The scriptural phrase is to dance "before the Lord" (2 Sam. 6:14,16). Dancing is not something the Holy Spirit makes you do. It is an act of obedience and love. If we had to be "in the Spirit" to dance, we would have to be "in the Spirit" to worship or sing or lift our hands. The Bible mentions "dancing before the Lord" just as we are to "play music before the Lord" (2 Sam. 6:21, NKJV).

Worship with movement is an attitude of love expressed actively. It is not a weird spirit-trance that someone gets into and then loses all control of his or her body.

Expressive movement is an act of our wills in worship to the Lord. We, not the Holy Spirit, set our feet to dancing and lift our hands to the Lord. We sing our praises to God with all our hearts. The Holy Spirit does not make us do any of these.

Movements are invested with meaning because human beings have bodies and spirits. For example, kneeling signifies penitence or humility, while bowing is an act of

63

honor or submission. Skipping expresses joy.

Christian liturgical dance performs two major functions: 1) It tells a story, and 2) It gives bodily shape to gratitude or joy.

For example, dance has been used to accompany and illustrate biblical readings. In this setting, dance has the ability to proclaim the gospel or comment on a prayer, a psalm or a song. It can produce peace and promote participation by enabling each person to express his or her worship totally. It can unify the spiritual and physical aspects of the human nature in a sacramental way.

In a public worship service, dance can be used in several ways. It can be the spontaneous expression of each believer when there is a spirit of joy in his or her heart. Worship leaders should be definite or assertive in leading the congregation in this form of celebratory expression. Then the response of joy can go somewhere.

The other use of dance is in special presentations. The congregation may become inspired in worship and their hearts full of adoration by the choreographed worship movement. This would serve well as a call to worship. Often it requires a response.

If you have never expressed your love to the Lord in dance, I would encourage you to try. When I first attempted to dance before the Lord publicly, it was a little embarrassing.

The Sunday evening service had concluded. The pastor invited those who could stay to come to the front and celebrate the Lord. Being a member of the youth group, I felt all alone when the entire group went to the front of the church and danced as the worship team played songs of joy and praise. I was too "cool" to do what they were doing, though inside I envied them. They were smiling and looked very happy. What a contrast to my leaning on the pew in front of me as I stood alone, stubborn and under conviction. I knew the Lord wanted me to join them.

Finally I did. I jumped up on one foot and then on the other. I felt clumsy. While they were going up, I was coming down. This was especially embarrassing for a basketball player who had danced at many school functions. Not giving up, in a few moments I sensed an eruption of joy in my heart, and my frown turned to a smile. I had offered the sacrifice of joy.

Writing on the subject of whether "I" should dance, Jack Hayford said:

> You can always find a spiritual expert whose "second opinion" will justify yours:
>
> Well, some people just need a lot of exuberance. Others of us don't. (The implication is that mature people don't.)
>
> It's all a matter of a person's cultural background. You and I are culturally reserved. (The implication is that *reserved* is socially or culturally advanced.)
>
> You must watch out for emotionalism: It becomes so subjective and worship loses its objectivity in worshipping God and starts to center on man. (The theological concern for *God's glory* obviously makes this righteously unchallengeable.)
>
> I believe — don't you? — that everyone should worship God in his own way, and according to his own beliefs. After all, to do otherwise is...well, it's...it's uncivil. You know each of us worships God according to the dictates of his own heart.[4]

Not Culture-Based

When we gave our lives to Christ, He set us free from the sentence of eternal damnation, and great rejoicing was in order. In the same way, when the Israelites were delivered from Pharaoh and passed through their baptism in the Red Sea, they began to rejoice. The horses and the riders — their enemies — were swallowed in the sea by the hand of God. Deliverance caused rejoicing, which in turn initiated dancing.

> Miriam the prophetess, the sister of Aaron, took the timbrel in her hand; and all the women went out after her with timbrels and with dances (Ex. 15:20).

While Moses sang a prophetic song, his sister led the women in circle dances. The dances of the Israelites at the Feast of Tabernacles (Judg. 11:34) most likely consisted of circle movements with rhythmical steps and lively gestures. The women would beat out a rhythm on cymbals and triangles.[1]

A whole company of dancers skipped and leaped among the rocks and plants. They had been delivered from extreme bondage. They had a rebirth of faith in their God that resulted in a rebirth of worship expression.

This account of Miriam and the women dancing is the first mention of dancing in the Bible (Ex. 15:20). As far as we know, Israelites danced only for religious reasons.

> While the mode of dancing is not known in detail, it is clear that men and women did not generally dance together, and there is no real evidence that they ever did. Social amusement was hardly a major purpose of dancing, and the modern method of dancing by couples is unknown.[2]

Many Christians write off their involvement in expressive worship by saying, "Well, they were Hebrew, and that was their custom." Dancing may not be your ethnic expression, but perhaps it wasn't the Jews' ethnic expression at this time of history either. Just as we do, they worshipped in expressive movement as a result of seeing God move on their behalf. It didn't have to be a "cultural thing."

Dancing Through Resistance

In 1987 I was conducting a worship seminar in Jamiltepec, Mexico, in an unfinished church building. The seven-foot walls made of concrete blocks were thatched with banana leaves. Even with the temperature at a hundred degrees, the building was packed.

On this particular morning, a local worship team was playing, but there was not the usual atmosphere of rejoicing among the people. The people often clapped their hands and jumped or hopped as they worshipped. But not this morning. There seemed to be a spiritual resistance. This continued for about twenty minutes.

Then all of a sudden a young Indian boy jumped up from the front row and began to dance across the front of the church. He wore a simple white long-sleeved shirt and white drawstring pants with no decoration or buttons.

His dance was unique. In all of my travels I had never seen a worship movement like this. He would leap and fling his arms toward heaven at the same time. It was the most innocent movement of worship I had ever seen. Our spirits leaped inside us as we saw an example of how David must have danced in front of Israel.

The young man was dancing as if he were praying in intercession with an overtone of joy. There was a sense that this man was being obedient to the Lord. As he stamped and leaped in front of the church, a joy came over the rest of us. Men, women and children moved out into the aisles and filled the front. Almost everyone began to express themselves to the Lord with joyous movement. It continued for about forty-five minutes or more.

When the service ended, we looked for that boy so that we could speak to him, but we couldn't find him. We asked the church leaders who he was, but no one in the villages knew him. We wondered if we had been in the presence of an angel because of the countenance and pure expression of that exuberant dancer.

The Scripture's Invitation to Dance

Some say that because expressive worship is not mentioned in the New Testament it should not be employed in our worship.

But the Bible says that all Scripture is profitable for doctrine, reproof, correction and instruction in righteousness (2 Tim. 3:16-17).

That means that this exhortation in Psalms,

Sing to God, sing praises to His name; extol Him who rides on the clouds, by His name Yah, and rejoice (jump for joy) before Him (Ps. 68:4, parentheses added),

is as valid as John's words in Revelation:

Let us be glad and rejoice (jump with exceeding joy) and give Him glory (Rev. 19:7, parentheses added).

In addition, the New Testament often quotes the book of Psalms. If the writers of the New Testament considered the Psalms to be a valid guide for living, then we should also pay attention to the Old Testament.

Our basic consideration should be this: Is expressive movement taught as an act of worship in the Bible?

Dancing in the Old Testament

The Old Testament is filled with exhortations and examples about worshipping the Lord through dance.

David killed a bear and a lion with his hands when he was a child and went on to kill thousands in battle. Yet he was called the "sweet singer of Israel" and knew how to involve his body in wholehearted and whole-strength praise.

> Then David danced [whirled] before the Lord with all his might; and David was wearing a linen ephod. So David and all the house of Israel brought up the ark of the Lord with shouting and with the sound of the trumpet (2 Sam. 6:14-15).

What was it like for David to leap and whirl with all of his might in the presence of the Lord? Was it graceful? Did he take lessons from women dancing instructors?

Probably not. He was a man's man. His form of expression probably bore no resemblance to a French ballet, a contemporary jazz dance or country line dancing. It most likely was violent, wild jumping and whirling of his body. I imagine he looked like a huge football player running and jumping across the field with all his strength, totally focused on the Lord in worship, dancing only for God's pleasure.

Real men still worship like this — jumping and skipping while they play their guitars. Strong, masculine expressions of worship please the Lord.

> And it happened, as the ark of the covenant of the Lord came to the City of David, that Michal, Saul's daughter, looked through a window and saw King David whirling [stamping, springing about (wildly or for joy) — jumping, leaping, or skipping[5]] and playing music (1 Chr. 15:29).

Moffatt says David was whirling about and sporting.[6] This translation says he was dancing like a mad man. It must have been intense, wholehearted expression in praise to God.

God cursed those who opposed David's wholehearted dancing. When Michal spoke against David's dance, God made her barren (2 Sam. 6:23). Michal's kind of mocking attitude bears no life among believers.

I have always wondered why Michal was not celebrating the presence of God with the rest of Israel. Her carnal nature and her pride resisted this type of worship. When you have a revelation of the greatness and grace of God, you worship wholeheartedly without concern for who is watching you. Don't speak against someone who worships more wholeheartedly than you are accustomed to.

David explained his actions to Michal this way:

> It was before the Lord...therefore I will play music before the Lord. And I will be even more undignified than this, and will be humble in my own sight (2 Sam. 6:21b-22).

David's attitude was right because he danced "before the Lord." People who dance before the Lord do not care where they are when they dance. They can dance at the back of the congregation as well as at the front, in public or in private. Their dance is not to be seen by the people; it is "for the Lord."

David also insisted that he would be even more abandoned to the Lord in unrefined, expressive worship. He was not concerned with the dignity and protocol of men. He was dancing for his Lord.

David wrote about dancing in worship before the Lord in several psalms.

> You have turned for me my mourning into dancing;

You have put off my sackcloth and clothed me
with gladness (Ps. 30:11).

Let the righteous be glad;
Let them rejoice (jump for joy) before God;
Yes, let them rejoice (make mirth) exceedingly
(Ps. 68:3, parentheses added).

He has made a difference in our lives; therefore we
celebrate.

Leaping for Joy in the New Testament

It is true that the word *dance* is not described in the New
Testament as an act of worship very often. Yet in several
places a verb form is used that conveys the idea of *leaping*
for joy, which is certainly another example of expressive
movement.

Jesus commanded us to leap for joy when people hate us,
exclude us, revile us or speak evil against us for His sake.

Be glad in that day, and leap for joy, for behold,
your reward is great in heaven (Luke 6:23, NAS).

The Greek word for leaped here is *skirtao*, meaning "to
skip, jump, sympathetically move or leap for joy."[7]

John the Baptist also leaped for joy (*skirtao*) *because of*
the presence of Jesus. It happened when Mary was pregnant with Jesus and went to tell the news to her cousin
Elizabeth, who was pregnant with John.

When Elizabeth heard the greeting of Mary, the Bible
says that John "leaped in her womb; and Elizabeth was
filled with the Holy Spirit" (Luke 1:41). When Mary walked
into the room, I believe John danced for joy at the presence
of Jesus.

Acts 3 gives an account of a man leaping about after he

was healed by the power of God. He had been lame from birth and was carried every day to the temple gate called Beautiful. There he begged for money. When Peter and John came along they told him to rise up and walk in the name of Jesus Christ of Nazareth.

> [Peter] took him by the right hand and lifted him up, and immediately his feet and ankle bones received strength. So he, leaping up, stood and walked and entered the temple with them — walking, leaping, and praising God. And all the people saw him walking and praising God (Acts 3:7-9).

This man, joyous because of the miracle of healing, couldn't keep his feet on the ground. He leaped up and down as he walked into the temple.

> In that hour Jesus rejoiced in the Spirit (Luke 10:21).

The word *rejoiced* here means "to exalt, be glad and overjoyed." When one is overjoyed, that excitement is expressed emotionally and audibly. I believe that Jesus shouted, jumped up and down or expressed Himself in other visible ways as the Spirit caused Him to be overjoyed.

The same word for *rejoice* is used to describe the reaction of the Philippian jailer when Paul and Silas told him the good news.

> He rejoiced, having believed in God with all his household (Acts 16:34).

I believe you could *see* that this man was excited about what the Lord had done for him.

Where Did We Lose It?

Something more incredible than a physical healing has happened to those of us who know Christ as Lord and Savior. Christ reached down and lifted up a people who were crippled by sin and death and gave them the miracle of eternal life. What better reason to leap and praise God in full view of all the world? If a man who gets physically healed in the New Testament can jump up and down in the temple, then those who are spiritually healed should feel free to glorify God just as exuberantly.

I used to look at these examples of dancing and leaping in Scripture and wonder why they ever died out in the church. Later I learned that expressive movement never disappeared entirely. But some powerful cultural influences inhibited it for many years. 🍂

8

HOW DANCING
GOT A BAD
REPUTATION

A LOT has changed in the Pentecostal/charismatic community since the days spoken of in the following paragraph. Expressive movement is now gaining acceptance with many individuals and churches.

In the early 1970s Oral Roberts had been invited to speak at the annual Full Gospel Business Men's Fellowship in Washington, D. C. Oral had brought with him his new student singing group, the World Action Singers. All went well until their final song — a hymn. As the group sang "O Worship the King," they began to move. Not much.

But it was obviously a well-rehearsed choreographed step. As they shifted to the left and right,
a muted gasp went up from the congregation.
Few if any had ever seen movement incorporated
as part of worship. Aside from the raising and
clapping of hands, there was among evangelical,
Catholic and Pentecostal Christians an unwritten
law that said movement was...forbidden.[1]

The question is: Why was there so much resistance? The
answer begins with the very earliest years of the church.

Borrowed Is Bad

In the earliest days of the church, dancing crossed over
into Christian worship from the Jewish tradition. Processions, accompanied by male and female dancers, seem to
have been part of the Hebrew concept of sacred dancing
(Ps. 68:25; Jer. 31:13). This became a part of Christian
public worship, where solemn choir processions of young
men and women moved in time with sacred music.[2] This
showed a correct understanding of the value of the Old
Testament in a Christian's life.

However, as the church became more legalistic, such
movement was eliminated. Leaders were afraid that sacred
dancing might seem worldly or might even encourage
weak Christians to become part of sinful practices. Except
for rare instances, all forms of body movement in worship
were prohibited.[3]

Church leaders also justified condemning the practice
because of the fact that dancing was "borrowed" from Juda-
ism and other groups such as pagan cults and heretical
sects, although some took place in church buildings, particularly at the shrines of martyrs. In addition, dance among
the pagans had become a degraded pastime and was even
condemned by educated pagans.[4]

The problem was that the church was in a reactive mode instead of an obedient one. It reacted to outside pressures rather than being obedient to the Lord.

Mind Makes Right

Intellectualism also had a chilling effect on worship. Both Jews and Christians were influenced by the Greek system of thought proposed by Plato (c. 427-347 B.C.). It said that there is a world above the material world and that men could know this realm only by reason. In other words, man could understand and worship higher things only with his mind.

Worship to the Greek rationalist was the correct observance of ritual performed in the correct form of mind.[5]

Many people concluded that worship had to be understood before it could be experienced.

During the Dark Ages, the teachings of Thomas Aquinas (c. 1225-1274) reinforced this emphasis on the intellectual. His perspective was that though man was fallen, the mind of man was not affected by the fall. A Christian could therefore learn from the intellectual ideas of non-Christians.

Aquinas reintroduced the thoughts of Aristotle, one of Plato's students, into the church. He used reason in the service of revelation (scholasticism). When reason invalidates biblical or Holy Spirit revelation, then it is out of order. The Bible is a book of experiences as well as a book of doctrine. Theology came out of experience. After encountering the divine, one receives revelations. But the Spirit revelation must be consistent with biblical revelation. There has to be an absolute. The Word of God is truth.

Some students of history believe Aquinas's work led to the Renaissance and the Enlightenment, periods which brought great renewal in art and culture, even dance, drama and music. But imbedded in it all was the Greek rational approach to spiritual things. Worship and spirituality remained intellectual. Understanding God was the highest goal of man. God was an object to be studied.

These modes of thought have affected worship in Western Christianity. "Thought comes before action" and "Understanding comes before involvement" are concepts that have flavored our worship and kept us stoic and reserved. Conservatism and restraint have been highly regarded among believers in the church for millennia.

Acceptance Began With the Puritans

Expressive movement in worship through the Middle Ages was not very common, although social dances occurred in the churches, particularly at the times of great festivals. Even the reformation churches were not very open to the idea of using your body in worship in the dance.

Surprisingly, the group that began to accept dancing in worship was the Puritans around the early 1700s. The dancing had to follow two basic guidelines: 1) men danced with men and women with women, and 2) it brought glory to God and drew others to worship with godliness.

This was a renewal in worship. Passionate hearts found new expressions of worship to the Lord, though not all Puritans accepted dance in worship.

The Shakers felt the same way in the late eighteenth and early nineteenth centuries. Their services often consisted entirely of dancing. They believed that dance was a gift of the Holy Spirit that was not to be neglected. They saw it as a natural impulse of joy suitable to the end times.

The Shakers compared themselves to the prodigal son whose return was celebrated with music and dancing (Luke 15:21). They contended that worship should not be passive but very much active. They felt that the whole body should be used to praise the Lord, not just the vocal cords. They believed that when the congregation danced together, they experienced a unity that was symbolic of the church's unity.

They saw that dancing encouraged the use of natural aptitudes and affirmed equality between men and women. It released the feelings of the believers as expressed in the songs. The processional dance to them spoke of the Christian pilgrim on the road to the heavenly Jerusalem, identifying with the way of the cross in a triumphal march against the forces of darkness.

During this time, however, other groups that were still rooted in Greek thought continued to reject expressive movement, including some groups of Puritans, Anglicans and other Protestants. Their teachings were strongly rationalistic and in some cases based on scholasticism. Many did not believe in the use of musical instruments, dance, vestments or emotions in any form in Christian worship.

Pentecostal and Charismatic Dancing

The Holy Spirit brought a rebirth of dance in the church at three points in time:

1. The Pentecostal movement, which started with a revival in Los Angeles in the early 1900s and had worship characterized by vocal expression, maximum participation, speaking in tongues and dancing.[6]

2. The Latter Rain Movement, beginning around 1948.

3. The charismatic renewal, starting in the 1960s.

In short, starting at the turn of the century, and especially after World War II, dancing became used more and more often in liturgical worship services.

Jamie Buckingham, a beloved leader in the charismatic renewal, described some of the major steps in the development of expressive movement:

Expressive movement in worship was found at the Camps Farthest Out meetings in the 1950s.

CFO leaders began teaching what was known as "devotion in motion." Small groups were encouraged to portray in motion such hymns as "Open My Eyes That I May See" and "When I Survey the Wondrous Cross."[7]

In 1958 the Sacred Dance Guild was founded in the United States.

In the mid-1970s, Merv and Merla Watson from Jerusalem began traveling with the dance troop Shekinah, doing choreographed and expressive dancing. Worship leaders such as Dave and Dale Garrett from New Zealand taught "upper body movement."[8]

Gradually churches experimented. Charismatics and Pentecostals began dancing in churches and conferences across the nation. Some said that their enthusiastic dancing in place to the rhythm of lively choruses looked like a "charismatic two-step." Yet it was an exuberant expression of joy.

Charismatic Episcopalians occasionally allowed an interpretive dance as they worshipped during the Eucharist. Churches formed dance groups. Men and women rehearsed Jewish or circle dances, helping to lead worship in Hebraic costumes.[9]

Expressive movement also became accepted overseas. Dancing occurred during a mass at the opening of the Metropolitan Cathedral of Christ the King in Liverpool in 1967.[10] In the late 1970s, at a convocation of Anglican bishops in England, a number of bishops from around the world, dressed in full regalia, danced before the Lord at the high altar in Canterbury Cathedral.[11] The Christ Dance Fellowship of Australia was founded in 1978.[12]

Expressive Movement Today

Today, some churches have expressive-movement choirs that are used side-by-side with singing choirs. These dance groups are to inspire worship visually and not be an end in themselves.

I will never forget the first time I saw a processional of movement in worship. I was in a church in Santa Ana, California, in the late 1970s. The building was so full that my wife and I stood at the back.

Through the door behind me I could see the dancers preparing to come in. They were weeping and praying. I later found out they had fasted for seven days in preparation for this one act of worship. When they walked down the aisle to the music, the sweet atmosphere of worship touched my heart. The dancers were smiling through their tears. Every movement of their bodies was calculated worship to God.

Dance is more than performing rehearsed steps; it is an extension of the attitude of our hearts.

Other forms of expressive worship used in churches today include drama, mime and banners.

Conclusion

Some have said that worship in motion has come to stay. Whether this will be true or not, the principles of true biblical worship need to be underscored and practiced. We do not need to understand with our minds before we worship. We must simply obey.

Praise Him with the timbrel and dance (Ps. 150:4).

As we reincorporate expressive movement into our worship, our challenge will be to keep our focus on Christ and not on what we're doing. When we keep our focus right, then our worship is filled with a sense of awe and wonder. ❧

9

AWE
AND
WONDER

I WAS leading worship at the International Worship Leaders' Institute in Dallas, Texas, a few years ago. As we sang, "Take me in to the Holy of Holies," a key line in the song "Take Me In," I fell to my knees on the platform and wept. My heart had touched something in the Lord that broke me. I longed to draw near to the holy One. I had approached the unapproachable, and it touched me deeply.

Sometimes our Spirit-filled worship becomes focused on the external acts of worship, and we lose the awe and majesty of our worship. Unintentionally, the worship of our great God becomes casual and familiar.

Our recent freedom of expression seems like the culprit that distracts our hearts and minds from the Lord. This is not an indictment against the use of expression in worship, but a recognition of a human problem. When we love the Lord with all our souls (emotions) and strength (physical actions), we must also remember to love Him with all our hearts and all our minds.

With the introduction of more contemporary and varied expressions in our worship services, it is easy to get caught up in *how* we worship instead of *who* we worship. There are so many things that call for our attention — the musical punches and riffs, the intriguing harmonies and interesting arrangements, the movement of the expressive worshippers, the praise choir and so on. Sometimes it is easy to focus on the steps of the dance instead of the One for whom we are dancing.

However, distractions have always been a problem in the church. When something is new, we open our eyes and listen excitedly to what is occurring. When we have seen and heard it for awhile, we can settle back down, close our eyes, raise our hands in the air and focus once again on the Lord. How each of us responds to this kind of situation in worship will demonstrate the level of our discipline and maturity.

The danger is that sometimes we never close our eyes again and enter into worship. We just keep looking at what is going on around us. That is when worship becomes superficial, and we are deprived of the awesome presence of God.

We could lose our spirit of worship and our ability to connect with the Lord through superficial worship. But I believe there are things we can do to keep the awe and wonder in our worship.

Avoid Being Goal-Oriented

Some Pentecostal and charismatic believers attend public worship services with an attitude of getting something out of the service rather than giving something to the Lord. Our attitude and, therefore, our motivation are self-serving. Sometimes we want to get as much as we can out of the service, like a fast-food restaurant, rather than give as much as we can.

I remember one time when a man stopped me before a service and asked, "Who is leading worship?"

I told him the name of the person.

"Great!" he responded. "I really get a blessing when he leads."

Notice the emphasis on "I" and "get" in his explanation.

How many times have you asked, "Who is preaching today?" or "Who is leading worship?" We need to ask ourselves if it really makes a difference.

If we worship because it pays, it won't pay. As A. W. Tozer wrote, "Whoever seeks God as a means toward desired ends will not find God. God will not be used."[1]

Remember that we are coming together for a worship *service*. The word *service* means "to give for the benefit of another." We serve the Lord in worship whether we get anything out of it or not.

When we come to a worship service only to get a healing or a blessing or a word or a prayer, our motives are wrong. We come together to honor Christ. We come together to bless Jesus. We come to *give* as much as possible to the Lord.

Of course, the Lord will have compassion when we have a need, but coming to church just to "get" something will make our worship man-centered instead of Christ-centered. Our call as Christians is clearly to Christ-centered worship.

Focus on Christ

In the Old Testament, worship was the result of an action of God. For example, the exodus event resulted in spontaneous song and dance as Moses and Miriam led Israel in praise to God for the victory over Pharaoh. Christian worship is centered on an event as well — the resurrection and ascension of Christ. We call this the Christ event.

The Scriptures show that Christ is the central Person of the Bible. The written Word revolves around Him who is the living Word. He is the hub of the wheel of truth, and all truths are as spokes relating to Him. Speaking prophetically of Christ, David wrote, "In the volume of the book it is written of me" (Ps. 40:7, KJV).

Therefore, our worship today demonstrates the living, dying and rising of Christ. It celebrates Christ's victory over evil and the doom of Satan. It speaks of God's saving action in sending Jesus Christ.

The event of Christ is the only event in human history that promises eternal life, meaning and purpose. These miracles invoke passionate and heartfelt praise. Worship is really a celebration of the work of Christ. In this kind of worship, God breaks in to touch our lives and renew us.

Christ-driven worship cannot be goal-driven worship. We do not worship for what we want to achieve but for the Person who deserves worship.

However, when Christ is the center of worship, all our goals are achieved. Christ-centered worship educates, heals, delivers, inspires and is most enjoyable. When we worship Him, we find His presence revealed. He comes near and becomes evident. And when He is present, He acts. It is in this kind of worship that we are most gratified and fulfilled.

A couple came to me at a worship seminar in Buenos Aires, Argentina. They were crying. The interpreter told me that the man had seen a vision while we were worshipping. He said he saw what looked like Christ sitting on a throne. He could not see the Lord's face because the light coming from Him was too bright. The man said that Christ stood up when we worshipped.

The man's wife, who at that time was in another place in the auditorium, said she saw a vision as well. She saw a throne that was empty because the Lord had stood up to see our worship. When they shared that, they began to weep, for it had meant so much to them. The Lord, the focus of our worship, stood up to let us know He was pleased.

Regain a Historical Perspective

We as Pentecostals and charismatics often do not have an historical perspective of worship. As a result, we believe worship that is Spirit-filled, vibrant, wholehearted and expressive (or whatever you call our worship) began with us. When we have the concept that "real" worship started in the 1970s, then the wonder and majesty of the historical aspect of worship are somewhat lacking.

I remember standing in the great cathedrals of northern Europe and seeing the murals of angels and drawings of Christ. The stained glass and high archways, the statues and the lofty altars, made my heart want to burst out in chorus with the ancient praise that had gone on before in those great halls of worship.

Vibrant worship has been part of the church since its conception. At times it became legalistic and cold. But the Lord has been building His church in worship. For two thousand years the Holy Spirit has been at work in believers' lives, bringing them to Christ-centered and Christ-revealed worship. Part of this book is devoted to showing you how that journey of worship affects our worship today.

Bring Back Furnishings That Point to Christ

When I visited those great cathedrals in Europe, I began to realize how little the furnishings of our modern North American churches did to inspire worship.

We no longer have beautiful stained-glass windows with ornate pictures representing Scriptures about Christ or the apostles. Many churches have done away with the elegant banners on the walls that reminded us of the greatness of our God. Some do not even have a cross. And some of our churches do not look much different from stores or office buildings.

All the furnishings I have mentioned are important aspects of enhancing the awe and mystery of our worship — just as the furnishings of the temple inspired worship among the Israelites.

Our sanctuaries must have the look and feel of sacred places where God can be found — apparent to both religious and nonreligious eyes.

In balance, let me reiterate that Christ said God is not concerned with *where* we worship but with *how* we worship (John 4:20-23). Making our church buildings look more sacred and Christian is simply a way of inspiring the believers and nonbelievers to worship. It helps restore wonder to our worship.

Enlarge Our Vision

I remember one time when we were worshipping through song at a worship institute in Milwaukee. The songs that the leader chose portrayed so powerfully the kingdom of God in lyric and spirit that many were overwhelmed by the sense of Christ's supremacy and majesty.

I was standing in the front row with my eyes closed when I heard a strange sound. I looked down the row to where my pastor, Glen Roachelle, had been standing. I saw him stretched out on the floor face down with his arms above his head and his palms flat. It looked as if he was weeping. My immediate response was to do the same. His action matched the longing in my own spirit.

The awe and wonder of God's revealed presence overcame us. Our response was prostration in His presence. We had a new revelation of His supremacy and majesty.

The most important way to restore awe and wonder in our worship is to seek a new revelation of the One we are worshipping. The mightiest thoughts that the mind can contain are the thoughts of God. When we see who He is, we naturally surrender ourselves to worship.

In the next chapter I describe the awe-inspiring, worship-worthy attributes of our unmatchable Lord. If you have never before meditated on the Lord's attributes, you will experience a brand-new sense of urgency and necessity in worship. You'll be captivated by His worth! ❦

10

CAPTIVATED BY HIS WORTH

ONE ASSOCIATE pastor of a charismatic church told me he had never heard a sermon like the one I had preached at the International Worship Leaders' Institute in Dallas. His comment surprised me.

The message was on the character of God and it was titled "The God We Worship." When I was preaching, there was a strong spirit of worship. I could feel people wanting to explode in exaltation. Why? Because the message declared the character and attributes of God.

My point is that sometimes we have a small view of God. The more we see Jesus high and lifted up, the greater rebirth of worship we will experience. What is our transcendent Lord like? What should our enlarged view of Him show us?

Ezekiel saw visions of God. He was looking at things that no language could describe, so he used the language of resemblance — "their appearance was like..." (Ezek. 1:13). The closer he approached the throne, the less sure his words became. He was describing things he had not seen before. That is what it is like to be caught up with the Lord in vibrant worship.

The divine Being dwells in obscurity, hidden behind the cloud of unknowing. Because of the cloud, we cannot see God through our own understanding or feel Him by our emotions.

We really can't answer the question of what God is like. But we can answer this question: What has God revealed about Himself?

He Is Self-Existent

In the beginning was the Word, and the Word was with God, and the Word was God. He was in the beginning with God. All things came into being through Him; and apart from Him nothing came into being that has come into being (John 1:1-3, NAS).

God has no origin. This distinguishes that which is God from whatever is not God. Origin applies only to those things that are created.

When I was a child, I was lying on the grass in our front yard one evening, looking at the stars. My aunt, who was a missionary, was with me, and I asked her, "Where did God come from?" My grandmother overheard me from her rocking chair on the porch and was shocked that I would ask such a question. But haven't we all, in our simple way, thought about that deep theological question?

The answer to the question is that God came from no-

where. He lies beyond us, exists outside all of our catego-
ries and will not submit to the interrogation of our reason.
He is the "I am that I am" (Ex. 3:14, KJV).

No one can explain His existence. When we grasp the
grandeur of that concept, it inspires us to greater heights of
worship.

He Is Self-Sufficient

Whatever God is, and all that God is, He is in Himself. He
gives to all but receives nothing that He hasn't first given.

He has no need. To have need is to admit that He
is incomplete in His divine being. *Need* is a creature
word that cannot be spoken by the One who is the Creator.
He has a *voluntary* relationship to anything outside of
Himself and no *necessary* relationships to anything that is
not in Him. His interest in His creatures comes from His
sovereign good pleasure, not from any need those creatures can supply.

Therefore, He did not create us or the angels to meet an
unfulfilled need He has to be worshipped. He is not insecure and vain. To worship Him does not increase or add
anything to Him. He is not lacking something if we do not
worship Him.

As A. W. Tozer once said:

> We commonly represent Him as a busy, eager,
> somewhat frustrated Father hurrying about seek-
> ing help to carry out His benevolent plan to bring
> peace and salvation to the world...The God that
> works all things surely needs no help and no
> helpers. Too many missionary appeals are based
> upon this frantic frustration of Almighty God.[1]

God is the Being supreme over all. He cannot be ele-
vated. Nothing is beyond Him; nothing is above Him. Any

motion in His direction is elevation for the creature.

If every man on earth was an atheist, it would not affect God in the least bit. To believe in Him adds nothing to His perfection, and to doubt Him takes nothing away. No one can promote Him, so no one can degrade Him.

God exists for Himself, and man exists for the glory of God. The high honor of God is a reality in heaven and must fill the earth as well. He needs no one, yet He works through all those who have faith in Him. He created and maintains His creation in perfect order without need of anything or anyone. He is complete in Himself. To see God this way — the way He is — enhances our worship.

He Is Eternal

God never hurries. There are no deadlines against which God works. He does not have to save the world by the year 2000 to fulfill our prophecy charts. Time is His servant. The schedule of all creation is His schedule. The Scriptures say:

> Even from everlasting to everlasting, Thou art God (Ps. 90:2, KJV).

For God, everything that will happen has already happened. He sees the end and the beginning in one view. The *alpha* and *omega* are the same.

> I am God...declaring the end from the beginning, and from ancient times things that are not yet done (Is. 46:9-10).

God dwells in eternity, but time dwells in God. As C. S. Lewis noted:

> If you picture Time as a straight line along which

we have to travel, then you must picture God as the whole page on which the line is drawn. We come to the parts of the line one by one: we have to leave A behind before we get to B, and cannot reach C until we leave B behind. God, from above or outside or all round, contains the whole line, and sees it all.[2]

Outside of Christ, time is a devouring beast. But to us who believe, time is a kitten, licking our hands, waiting to fulfill its purpose.

He Is Infinite

The word *infinite* can be used of no one but God. He is measureless. We cannot speak of measure or amount or size at the same time we speak of God, for these tell of degrees, and there are no degrees in God. He is without growth or addition.

Everything that flows out of Him is infinite as well. The gift of eternal life is limitless. So the infinitude of God is in each finite believer.

The mercy of God is infinite. Where sin abounds, grace *much more* abounds (Rom. 5:20). Sin, the terror of the world, is relentless. But no matter how much sin is revealed, there is always more grace. It is infinite because He is infinite.

He is greater than all language, and no statement can express Him. Our most expressive songs only begin to describe Him. No lyric can contain all that He is. Our high, elegant utterances of praise and worship are trivialities in comparison to the holy One. But when the eternalness of God is portrayed in our worship services, it can cause a heart to worship more largely. Our view of God is enlarged.

He Is Immutable

God says of Himself, "I do not change" (Mal. 3:6). He never differs from Himself. Moral creatures go from worse to better or better to worse. They can change within themselves from immature to mature. But God cannot go in any of those directions. He does not vary.

God cannot change for the better. He is perfectly holy. He never has been less holy than He is now and has never been more holy than He is now. Any deterioration of His nature and being is impossible.

All that God is He has always been, and all that He has been and is, He will ever be. The slightest degree of change would make God no longer self-existent, self-sufficient or eternal.

His attitude toward us now is the same as it was in eternity past and will be in eternity future. This is a comforting thought. We do not need to wonder if we will find Him in a receptive mood when we worship Him. God never changes moods or loses affection or enthusiasm. God will not compromise or be coaxed. He cannot be persuaded to alter His word.

Nothing God has ever said about Himself will be modified, and nothing the prophets or apostles said about Him will be rescinded. If He inhabited the praise of believers in the past, He will dwell in our praise today. We do not have to persuade, coax, con or manipulate Him to do so. If we could make Him do something that is not of His choice, He would not be God as we have just described Him.

We cannot practice the presence of God in the sense that we produce His presence when we worship as if we're calling a genie out of a lamp. He dwells among our praises because He said He would (Ps. 22:3). Our efforts do not cause God to do anything He has not already promised He would do in Scripture.

We Pentecostals and charismatics sometimes have the notion that if we pray harder and perhaps louder, God will be more likely to answer our prayers. Does that mean we can cause God to do something He may not want to do? In the same way, praising louder or jumping higher in our dance does not mean that our worship is more acceptable or better.

He Is Sovereign

Who is mightier than the mightiest? Who is higher than the highest? From whom does God get advice? To which throne does He bow? There is none. He is the ceiling of all limits, goals and pursuits. One cannot be greater, mightier, stronger, more knowledgeable, faster or better than He. He is the top God.

Sovereignty means that God is free — free to do whatever He wills, anywhere He desires, at any time in order to carry out His eternal purpose. He has universal authority to do what He wants as He wants to. Why does He permit evil, accidents of saints, abortions of the unborn? Because He does, and He does not have to answer to anyone about it. God is sovereign, and He does what He knows is best.

Evil is permitted in carefully restricted areas of His creation, as a fugitive outlaw whose activities are temporal and limited in scope. He does this according to His infinite wisdom.

So freedom and sovereignty are combined in God and cannot contradict each other. When man chooses to do evil, he does not countervail the sovereign will of God. Rather he fulfills it in that God gives man the opportunity to choose.

God moves in a steady course on the sea of history, undisturbed and unhindered in His sovereignty toward the fulfillment of what He purposed in Christ before the world began.

He Is Transcendent

We cannot exalt God in our worship. But we declare His

exaltation. We cannot lift Him up because He is already lifted up. So we simply declare it.

Transcendent means that the Lord is exalted far above all creation, not only in distance but in quality of life. He is exalted to such a high level that human thought cannot comprehend the place.

> For thus says the high and exalted One
> Who lives forever, whose name is Holy,
> I dwell on a high and holy place (Is. 57:15, NAS).

Forever He stands apart in light unapproachable. He is as high above a single created cell as He is above an archangel. That's because the gulf is infinity.

Wouldn't it be strange, after feeling the fire of God's holy presence and hearing the words of His mouth, to come to earth and listen to some of the things Christians say? How empty our songs and how flat our sermons would seem. How you would burn to describe God to all in word and song. Would you want to write a song about anything less than theology? Would you want to do anything less than worship?

If you had experienced such a revelation of God, would you be content with superficial worship in the form of what some call "preliminaries"? Or would you burn to sing of the transcendent Lord you had just seen and heard?

Psalm 113:4-6 describes the transcendence of the God we worship.

> The Lord is high above all nations,
> His glory above the heavens.
> Who is like the Lord our God,
> Who dwells on high,
> Who humbles Himself to behold
> The things that are in the heavens and in the
> earth?

New Words

When we see the Lord so high and lifted up, we often find that our normal words fail to express what we see and feel. Saying "hallelujah" or "glory to God" is no longer adequate. Some of our words are overused and abused. I have asked the Lord to give me new words to declare His attributes in worship.

One day I went through a thesaurus finding alternative words for my familiar words. Now I use these in my declarative worship. For example,

Lord,
You are unrivaled, unparalled, unequaled and
   unsurpassed.
You are peerless, matchless, faultless and flaw-
   less. God, You are choice, fine, elite, splendid, marvelous, glorious, fabulous and
   wondrous.
Phenomenal, sensational, splendid, spectacular,
   majestic, fantastic and terrific is my King.

Your presence is amazing, awe-inspiring,
   astonishing, outstanding, stirring, stimulating
   and electrifying.
You are so large, grand, great, immense and
   massive.
You're magnificent, brilliant, radiant, resplendent
   and transcendent.

Your Person is superior, superb and sublime.
I have discovered You to be excellent, exquisite, exceptional, extraordinary, remarkable,
   incomparable, impeccable, irreproachable
   and unimpeachable.

There is absolutely none like You.
You stand alone.

Look at the way Paul described the wonders of God's character to the Ephesians:

> And [so that you can know and understand] what is the immeasurable and unlimited and surpassing greatness of His power in and for us who believe, as demonstrated in the working of His mighty strength, which He exerted in Christ when He raised Him from the dead and seated Him at His [own] right hand in the heavenly [places], far above all rule and authority and power and dominion, and every name that is named — above every title that can be conferred — not only in this age and in this world, but also in the age and the world which are to come.
>
> And He has put all things under His feet and has appointed Him the universal and supreme Head of the church, which is His body, the fullness of Him Who fills all in all — for in that body lives the full measure of Him Who makes everything complete, and Who fills everything everywhere [with Himself] (Eph. 1:19-23, AMP).

Reading a portion of Scripture like this causes your heart to arise in worship. One cannot read, listen or speak this kind of declaration of Christ's transcendence and not be inspired to worship Him. Revealing these attributes of God in our worship services brings a rebirth of worship into our lives.

Seeing God

When aspects of God's character are taught, preached, studied and sung, they will go a long way toward bringing us into a rebirth of worship. A high vision of God brings a higher ascent into worship.

We do not (and should not) imagine what God is like and worship Him through our imaginations. We worship Him as the Holy Spirit reveals Him to our seeking hearts. In that way, our worship is Spirit-inspired and Spirit-directed.

This often requires launching out in faith beyond our prepared songs and prayers to find the Spirit of God revealing the incomprehensible, to touch and taste the unapproachable (see Ps. 34:8).

I often bring this verse before the Lord in prayer:

Blessed are the *pure* in heart, for they shall see God (Matt. 5:8, italics added).

I ask the Lord for a pure heart so that I can see Him. A worshipper has not only a passionate heart, but also a pure heart. A heart that is after God has an innocence and cleanness about it. Oh, that all of our hearts would be like that!

The Holy Spirit can reveal the transcendent One through the Word of God. Reading the Holy Scriptures gives us a glimpse of the grandeur of our God. Worship often rises higher after the reading of Scripture, whether in our personal devotions or in a worship service — especially after the preaching. The response of worship in the hearts of people is more wholehearted after hearing the Word of God.

Have you ever been in a worship service or at home when you felt the unmistakable presence of the Lord? One of the most significant things there is to know about worship is that there is a purpose to His presence. In the next chapter we will discover four important things that happen in the presence of the Lord. ❦

11

THE PURPOSE
OF HIS
PRESENCE

HAVE YOU ever considered why the Lord shows His presence to His people? Have you ever been in His presence and not known why you were there? What does God want to do, if anything, when He reveals Himself?

I used to believe that we were to worship Him and not expect — or even look for — the benefits of His presence. I thought church leaders who felt the Lord's presence and immediately put Him to work were not focused on God in worship and were only "sheep-conscious." I assumed they were uncomfortable about being in God's presence be-cause they were always talking to the people, giving directions and not letting the people commune with God. Perhaps they themselves didn't spend much time with the Lord. In my heart I accused them of seeking God's hand for benefits, instead of seeking His face to know Him.

However, I have since learned that God has a purpose for revealing His presence in worship. The Scriptures show us that God has an eternal purpose in all that He does.

> Though they [children] were not yet born and had done nothing either good or bad, in order that *God's purpose of election might continue,* not because of works but because of his call (Rom. 9:11, RSV, italics added).

> In Him also we have obtained an inheritance, being predestined according to the *purpose of Him* who works all things according to the counsel of His will (Eph. 1:11, italics added).

> Who has saved us and called us with a holy calling, not according to our works, but *according to His own purpose* and grace which was given to us in Christ Jesus before time began (2 Tim. 1:9, italics added).

Everything that occurs in our lives works together for good to those that love God and to those who are the called "according to His purpose" (Rom. 8:28).

Recognizing His Purpose

When the Lord comes to us in our worship, it is often to make up for our human needs or inadequacies. In churches that worship, people's needs are being met because of God's evident power in their midst. Such power encounters change people's lives. I am not talking about using worship for our own end. Nor am I suggesting our worship be manipulated to serve our human wants. However, in true worship God desires to meet our needs and see us changed. It is clear that, with God, we are at the center of His concern, especially when we worship.

As Jack Hayford wrote:

> The Scriptures consistently show God calling His creatures to worship in His presence that He might release, redeem, renew and restore them.[1]

When we understand the purpose of His presence, then we can work with the Lord on His agenda and see more divine (supernatural) things happen. If God has a reason for revealing His presence, then we must discern what it is to the best of our ability and flow with Him.

At the same time, I want to mention that there are times when God may choose *not* to reveal His purpose. He may want to work outside our perceptive ability.

Now I want to describe for you several purposes that I have seen fulfilled in the presence of the Lord.

His Presence Brings Redemption

The Bible is clear that one of God's purposes in revealing Himself within praise is to redeem the lost.

> He has put a new song in my mouth, a song of praise to our God. Many shall see and fear — revere, and worship — and put their trust and confident reliance in the Lord (Ps. 40:3, AMP).

Vibrant worship directed to God provides a perfect environment for evangelism. When we sing the new song, in our praise and worship, *many* will see — not just a few. This is the same type of praise in which God dwells (Ps. 22:3).

101

Two things come to mind here. The first is that "many" will be affected by the new song and trust in the Lord. Could this kind of praise be a key to power encounters with God's presence that would result in many transformed lives?

When I was at a national worship conference in Calgary, Alberta, called Canada Arise, a twelve-year-old boy gave his heart to the Lord during the spontaneous singing of the new song. This occurred without any direction from the platform. No one gave an invitation to receive Christ. I may have never known what God had done in His presence if someone had not told me about the boy, and I had not talked to him. It made me wonder what other things may occur in the hearts and lives of believers during a worship encounter with God.

His Presence Brings Revelation

The second thing that strikes me about Psalm 40:3 is that many will "see." It does not necessarily mean they will see the new song but that they will *see*, or behold. I believe the presence of God that accompanies our worship causes us to see into a spiritual realm.

As Jack Hayford wrote:

> Worship is an opportunity for man to invite God's power and presence to move among those worshipping Him. When God moves in, then people are drawn to Christ. We have found that worship is the *pathway* and the *atmosphere* in which people — the saved and the unsaved alike discover
> their royal calling in Christ,
> their high destiny in life,
> their fullest personal worth and
> their deepest human fulfillment.[2]

I believe He reveals His thoughts to us in worship. He gives us impressions of what He is thinking about certain things.

> Many, O Lord my God, are...
> Your thoughts toward us...
> If I would declare and speak of them,
> They are more than can be numbered (Ps. 40:5).

The presence of God is often revealed to tell God's people something that will help them. Moses experienced that when God's presence passed in front of Him.

> The Lord descended in the cloud and stood with him there and proclaimed the name of the Lord. And the Lord passed by before him, and proclaimed, The Lord! the Lord! a God merciful and gracious, slow to anger, and abundant in lovingkindness and truth (Ex. 34:5-6, AMP).

Through His presence, the Lord spoke, proclaimed or revealed something very meaningful to Moses. God's presence passed by for a purpose: to let humankind know that God is full of grace and mercy.

The Scriptures say that the Lord spoke to Moses "just as a man speaks to his friend" (Ex. 33:11, NAS). The Lord still wants to speak to us.

In Psalm 29 the term *voice of the Lord* is used seven times in the context of giving the Lord glory and worshipping Him in the beauty of holiness. Our worship invites His presence. When He is present, He speaks. He speaks out of His revealed presence. It says that the voice of the Lord is powerful and breaks trees, splits lightning, strips the forest bare and causes deer to give birth, while those in the temple cry out, "Glory" (Ps. 29:1-11).

In His presence we hear the voice of the Lord, and lives are changed. We can rarely see what is going on in the supernatural realm, but we can see the results in the natural realm. If we did not worship, think about what would *not* happen.

His Presence Brings Joy

God comes to us in our worship to give us a divine impartation of joy. He anoints our heavy, burdened and failing spirits with the oil of joy (Is. 61:3). Gone are the concerns that burden us and the depression that darkens our spirits. We are free to soar in His presence.

> You will show me the path of life;
> In Your presence is fullness of joy;
> At your right hand are pleasures forevermore
> (Ps. 16:11).

There is exhilarating ecstasy in God's revealed presence. People become cheerful and glad once again. Their spirits are encouraged and brightened up.

Isaiah describes one of the purposes of the Spirit of God to be

> to grant [consolation and joy] to those who mourn in Zion — to give them an ornament (a garland or diadem) of beauty instead of ashes, the oil of joy for mourning, the garment [expressive] of praise instead of a heavy, burdened, and failing spirit (Is. 61:3, AMP).

The presence of God brings comfort and consolation to the mournful. What a precious fruit of worship!

His Presence Destroys the Works of the Devil

Shiloh Christian Fellowship in Oakland, California, felt

called by God to do something about city neighborhoods that were plagued by gang violence and crime. The musicians, youth and worship team from the church obtained permits to close certain streets and held block parties at which they gave away clothing and food and celebrated the Lord with praise and worship. The church won the favor of the community and became a friend to the inner-city residents.

The Oakland police department noticed a change in the neighborhood after the block parties. There was a definite decrease in gang crime and drug dealing. The church has received acknowledgments from the mayor of Oakland, the Oakland Police Department and then-president George Bush. Their story was told on "Geraldo" and "Good Morning, America." The block parties have been so successful that when the police have a problem with gang violence, they call the church to come and hold another block celebration.[3]

You see, the presence of God in worship has an effect on the spiritual atmosphere of a neighborhood. The Father of Lights causes darkness to flee. The spirit of violence and greed that causes people to commit violent crimes is overcome by the presence of the Lord that dwells in praise which is part of worship (Ps. 22:3). The spirits of terror are handicapped when the God of creation is near. The presence of the church as salt and light also strengthens the evidence of the Lord's presence because all believers are temples of the Holy Spirit.

I remember an account that Bob Fitts, director of worship for Youth With a Mission, shared with our staff about a time that he took a worship team to a high place of worship in Southeast Asia. While they were worshipping, an old idol fell over. Government workers came and tried to prop it up two or three times and failed. They decided to let it lie.

Was this coincidental, or did the worship of believers have an effect not only on the spirit world but on the natural realm as well, causing objects of demonic worship to fall down? I believe it was the praise in their worship that invoked the presence of God in that area. God's presence made a difference in the atmosphere.

One of the purposes of the Lord in sending His presence is to destroy the works of the devil. We see this demonstrated in the life of Jesus, who was a manifestation of the presence of God. The Bible says:

> The reason the Son of God was made manifest (visible) was to undo (destroy, loosen and dissolve) the works the devil [has done] (1 John 3:8, AMP).

John, the disciple closest to Christ, knew Jesus was revealed to destroy the devil's work. I believe there are times when we can discern that the purpose of God's presence is to bring victory over the work of Satan. I believe those are times when it is appropriate to do spiritual warfare in the presence of God.

The Power of His Presence

It's sad when a worship service never encounters the presence of the Lord, and the worshipper goes home unchanged. It's a form of worship without the power.

Use without correct purpose is abuse. I believe we need to be careful that we seek to know God's purpose for His presence whenever we worship. Then we can get past our song lists and orders of service and encounter His power.

I believe we will see more signs and wonders associated with worship as we seek the Lord for His purposes. This is just one of several positive trends I see developing in the worship of churches and individuals today. ❦

12

Trends
in Worship
Today

MILLIONS OF Christians have experienced a re-birth of worship in their lives and their congregations during the last two decades.

This metamorphosis has touched almost every nation and denomination. And it is beginning to explode into every ethnic group.

This worship renewal can be seen in the appearance of such phenomena as worship tapes. Ten years ago few people knew what a worship tape was. Today thousands of people every other month purchase tapes that feature live worship music. Now each record company wants its own line of worship tapes. Companies that already have their own series of worship tapes include Integrity Music, Maranatha! Music, Word Records and Music, Mercy Records and others.

Never before have there been magazines or encyclopedia exclusively on worship. Today we have at least two magazines: *Psalmist* (Kent Henry Ministries, St. Louis, Missouri) and *Worship Leader* (CCM Communications, Nashville, Tennessee).

More books are being produced on the subject, including a seven-volume encyclopedia on Christian worship.[1] It represents 650 contributing editors from almost all denominations, including Pentecostal and charismatic churches as well as nondenominational fellowships or circles of influence.

These developments represent pivotal and foundational changes in our contemporary worship. As I look at where we've come from and evaluate the features of public worship today, I see some very positive, exciting trends.

More Desire for God's Presence

As I conduct seminars throughout North America I have found an increasing desire among many Christians for an awareness of the presence of God. They are dissatisfied with a worship service that is routine and lacking spiritual power. Singing seven songs and preaching a forty-five-minute message is not sufficient if God's presence is not evident in our midst.

Even when a charismatic church has a praise band that plays all of the latest worship songs, there can still be a lack of the presence of God.

In a worship service that is routine and mechanical — having correct form but lacking divine power — the Lord does not speak. He is not revealed or experienced by the worshippers. They go through the motions but do not touch the supernatural. When the presence of God is experienced and encountered, then we can discern what the Lord wants to do in the service.

As a result, many church leaders often allow one or two opportunities during a worship service for people to respond to the revealed presence of God. People may come forward to the altar or respond in prayer to what the Lord is saying.

Worshipping churches seek to develop a worship that is open to the supernatural, aware of mystery and committed to the participation of all.

More Participation

For years one of the problems of our evangelical worship was the passive nature of the congregation. We were to sit and watch. Our only role was to sing along with the music of the organ and the piano and to give an offering. We were spectators and not participants.

Today in all kinds of evangelical, denominational and nondenominational churches, worship is much more participatory. We have learned that worship is a verb. It is not something done for us but by us.

Have you ever been in a worship service where it seemed as if the pastor controlled everything? I become frustrated in those situations because I long to participate, to be involved. When I am given instructions every few minutes, I feel manipulated, like a lowly private at boot camp. Worship is no longer my personal, unique gift to the Lord.

It is a sad thing when the preacher and the worship leader become the surrogates for worship. Many people leave the service assuming they have worshipped but feeling dissatisfied in their spirits because they did not initiate or express worship that was of their choice.

When we are not participating, our spirits can't mature. They become dysfunctional, weak and shriveled up from lack of use. I believe we sense a need to participate — to see, hear, feel, taste, smell and move as we worship our God.

Platform ministries are merely prompters and facilitators for the congregation's worship. The congregation's worship is the center point and the most important ingredient of corporate worship services.

I distinctly remember being invited to speak at a Southern Baptist church in South Carolina two years ago. It was a Sunday morning worship service. Everyone was in their finest clothes. When the music started, a man dressed in a Hebraic costume came down the aisle with his hands raised, skipping to the joyful music. Several in the congregation also danced joyfully. I was taken aback; I had not expected this freedom of expression in a Southern Baptist church.

This congregation also insisted I go to the park with them that afternoon and worship among the unsaved. So, with curiosity, I joined them in song and procession as we skipped among the lovers in the park, glorifying our Lord among the heathen. It reminded me of the words of David:

> Therefore I will give thanks to You, O Lord,
>   among the Gentiles,
> And sing praises to Your name (2 Sam. 22:50).

As we participate more — and watch less — we find fresh joy and meaning in the worship of the Lord.

More Spontaneous

In reaction to the rigidity of worship in the past, many groups of churches are placing an emphasis on worship that is more spontaneous. The worship services are less structured and have moments when the congregation can express, without prompting, their own worship to the Lord.

There are also more times of waiting on the Lord at certain moments in the service. Acknowledging the presence of God — rather than just talking to each other about Him — is a key to warm Christian worship. This emphasis is occurring in more and more circles, including traditional denominations.

Though many people feel more secure singing familiar songs of worship, greater numbers are seeing the importance of extemporaneous expressions of worship.

More Vertical

I have noticed that some of our songs have changed. Twenty years ago, I remember singing mostly songs about what the Lord has done for us and about heaven. The focus was largely on the believer and the benefits of being a Christian.

Then the Lord gave the church such songs as "All Hail King Jesus," "Thou Art Worthy" and "I Exalt Thee." These were the beginning of an influx of songs that caused the believer to sing *to* the Lord instead of *about* Him. They helped to direct our hearts in vertical worship — not just horizontal communication.

It's important to listen to the words of the songs we sing. Many songs are about the Lord but are directed to others. These songs serve a purpose of proclamation, but songs directed *to* the Lord do a better job of helping our spirits ascend to a God-consciousness. Words focused on the Lord bring a "face-to-face" encounter more than words about Him.

The Question of Liturgy

Another important trend is the way some Pentecostal and charismatic churches are incorporating early methods of Christian worship into their services, which we discuss in the next chapter. Some people may argue that this trend is a step backward, but I believe these worship methods can bring a sincere, worshipping heart closer to the Lord. ❦

PART II

FOUNDATIONS
OF
WORSHIP

13

THE
REBIRTH OF
LITURGY

COMING FORWARD to partake of communion was an awkward liturgical practice for me at first. Our church, Metroplex Covenant Church in Colleyville, Texas, asks the members of each family to come forward together and take communion with an elder at the front. I was uncomfortable being in front of the rest of the congregation. I couldn't hide in the pew. But it made the Lord's supper more personal and interactive since we prayed and thanked the Lord for what He had done for us as a family.

In the last few years many charismatic churches have had a rebirth of interest in church tradition. They are taking a closer look at the liturgies that have been used for two millennia. Those who are interested are not necessarily ready to become liturgical, but in liturgy they see a rich tradition, heritage, order and content.

I believe this renewed interest indicates a desire for more substance and context in charismatic worship. It produces a convergence of worship styles that has been rooted in the Scriptures, developed throughout church history and mixed with a passion for God's presence. As Robert Webber, author and proponent of this trend, points out:

> Worshipping churches respect their own tradition, are in dialogue with the worship tradition of other churches, and draw from the church's worship practices throughout history.[1]

Some say the formal liturgical expressions of worship are too mechanical and remove the personal participation from the people. Others argue that these forms of worship — prayer books, processionals, weekly Eucharist, and so on — are too structured and confining.

Often when we think of liturgical worship we think of a fixed order, written prayers, classical music, candles and robes. We complain that it is ritualism, dead orthodoxy and vain repetition.

People are discovering that liturgy was not meant to be a closed order with no room for spontaneity. Rather it is a guide, taking the worshippers by the hand and leading them through a worship experience that is Christ-centered and well-rounded.

Almost every segment of the church has been guilty of prejudice or bias against worship traditions that are different from their own. This has separated the body of Christ for a long time. We did not appreciate other forms of worship because we did not understand them. Today, the hunger for a vibrant rebirth of worship is overcoming our desire to keep to ourselves.

115

A spirit of oneness is bringing the church together in new experiences of worship. When believers everywhere lift their spirits in worship and wonder to focus on the majesty and holiness of God, they experience a spiritual unity. This is described in Ephesians 4:3 where Paul urged the church to "keep the unity of the Spirit in the bond of peace."

Worshipping churches are drawing from the traditions of church history as well as from Scripture. Central issues are the work of Christ and a recognition that the Word and the communion table proclaim Him.

What is happening in this regard in the body of Christ seems to occur without any connections or motivation from certain parts of the church. It is obviously something that the Lord is doing in our time — breaking down prejudices, bringing people together through worship and giving us an historical perspective. Some believe that the future will be characterized by a blending of traditional and contemporary worship that will bring new life and vitality to our worship experience.

The Problem of Missing Out on History

The church of the Lord has deep roots in history because He who holds time in His pocket used it to shape our worship. As Americans, however, we tend to be ahistorical. We are naive because we are young as a nation. We are more interested in the "now" — the experience of our current existence.

Unfortunately, this is true also in local churches. Many charismatic churches are a result of a succession of breakaways or church splits. They follow a constant pattern of starting over again and do not have much respect for parental history.

This attitude often caused the charismatic church to cut itself off from the rich tradition God has given the church and the collective spiritual contributions of His people throughout the ages. At the same time, our vision of Him was diminished.

The Holy Spirit's direction to the church during the early years is foundational to our worship today. To ignore that would bring heresy into our worship. Robert Webber commented:

> The same Fathers who hammered out the authority of Scripture, wrote the great creeds, developed the disciplines of spirituality, and clarified the ethics of the church are the Fathers through whom the Spirit still delivers the keys to our understanding and practice of worship.[2]

Yet the Holy Spirit did not stop speaking after the apostles died. He has been moving and inspiring Spirit-filled worship for two thousand years. To deny that would be to say that He has not worked in church history.

A Pilgrimage of Discovery

Since the first convert to Christ in the first days of the church, we — the body of Christ — have been on a pilgrimage of discovery of the fullness of our Lord. In that journey we have discovered what it is to worship the One who redeemed our lives and changed our destiny forever. That unfolding revelation of truth is ever increasing our growth to maturity.

Those who say, "We have never worshipped that way before," only look at their own experiences and do not see the big picture of church history. What the Holy Spirit has been doing in bringing the church into wholehearted, vibrant, expressive worship over the last two thousand years has been phenomenal. The stoic few who say, "We're not ready for that," cannot stop it because the Holy Spirit's mission is to bring the church to the maturity Christ desires in our worship.

God's Word says that the church is a spiritual temple, erected to God's glory and created to worship Him (1 Pet. 2:5). The main function of the temple is the worship of the Lord Jesus Christ. It is her calling, her focus and her destiny.

We are holy priests who offer up spiritual sacrifices acceptable to God through Jesus Christ. No act is more central to the Christian life. Worship gives rhythm and structure to the Christian's life; it is the heartbeat of congregational life. Worship is the first act of a new church, and in hard times it's the last "program" to be cut — and when it's cut, the congregation ceases to exist.

Of course, by now it's obvious that Christian worship didn't begin with the charismatics or the Pentecostals. We are not detached from the historical church, nor are we a complete fulfillment of it. Our worship is incomplete without the perspective of what has been done through the whole church age. So how can we learn from the past?

Fitting Into the Big Picture

An historical overview of the church's journey in worship will shed light on the significance of where we are in our worship. It will let us see the big picture and how we fit.

We have a unique vantage point to be able to look through two millennia of worship and find the thread of truth in all of that. Finding that plumb line then helps us to redefine our philosophy of worship so that we can further the rebirth of worship in our hearts.

Another principle to keep in mind as we look through church history is that we not allow our worship to be defined by current cultural norms to the extent that worship loses its meaning, as it did periodically in the past. We can learn from what went astray in the expression and emphases of worship in the last two thousand years.

Finally, I believe that the church of today is enriched by continuing some of the most meaningful acts of worship from church tradition. An excellent example is the Christian calendar. It's absolutely foreign territory for some charismatics and Pentecostals, and it may seem rather routine and meaningless for some in mainline churches. But following different seasons of worship in the Christian calendar can greatly assist our worship. 🍏

14

THE
CHRISTIAN
CALENDAR

WHAT IS the purpose of a holiday? Think of Veteran's Day as an example. Instead of remembering those who fought in wars a little bit every day, we choose one day of the year to focus corporately on what they have done. The gesture of a holiday is used to give a certain group of people honor for what they have done.

In the same way, the Christian calendar sets up a cycle of corporately remembering what Christ has done for us. Special observances for Epiphany, Advent or Pentecost help us honor what the Lord has done for us.

The great advantage of using the calendar to guide liturgical celebration over the year is that proper focus is given to all aspects of the Christ event in a balanced way.

IMPORTANT EVENTS IN THE CHRISTIAN CALENDAR	
Advent	four Sundays prior to Christmas
Christmas	December 25
Epiphany	the closest Sunday to January 6
Lent	forty weekdays before Easter
Holy Week	the week before Easter
Easter	between March 23 and April 25
Pentecost	seventh Sunday after Easter

Lest you think this is beginning to sound Catholic, remember that holidays on the church calendar were part of Christian worship prior to the establishment of the Roman Catholic church. These forms of worship are as old as the Lord's church is. They are pre-Catholic, pre-Baptist, pre-Pentecostal and pre-charismatic. Here are the roots of our worship.

The Church Year

The most common term for the celebrations of the year in the Christian church is the *church year.* The oldest evidence of the church year is found in Paul's first letter to the Corinthians, which was written in 55 A.D. at the end of Paul's three-year stay in Ephesus (compare 1 Cor. 16:5-9; Acts 20:31). Paul referred to "Christ, our Passover" and encouraged the people to "keep the feast" (1 Cor. 5:7-8). But when early Christians observed this holy day, they did not celebrate Israel's deliverance from Egypt. Instead, they fasted to commemorate the sufferings of Jesus, the true Passover Lamb.

The source of the church year was the life, death, resurrection, ascension and second coming of the Lord Jesus Christ. Two of these major events took place during Jewish celebrations — the Passover (Christ's death) and Pentecost (His ascension took place a week before Pentecost). I be-

121

lieve the timing of events in Christ's life was God's deliberate choice.

The church year was a vital part of worship until the Reformation. The Reformers discontinued it because of the abuses attached to it during the late medieval period. So the good aspects of the church year were lost with the bad.

Today I believe we can observe the church calendar in an unadorned way that celebrates the major events of Christ's life among us. This would be similar to what the early church did.

Advent

The first place to begin in the church year is at Christ's birth. *Advent* means "coming" or "arrival." It represents the time preceding the birth of Christ.[2] In the sixth century it was the six weeks before Christmas and marked the beginning of the church year, although it was established after other parts of the year. Fasts occurred on Monday, Wednesday and Friday of each week. Eventually the Roman church reduced Advent to four Sundays.

The purpose of this celebration for worshippers today is to prepare for the coming of the Lord. It celebrates two aspects: 1) the first coming of Christ as a babe in Bethlehem and 2) His second coming. It helps believers recognize God's visitation in their lives today. Worship the Lord at this time for His interest and participation in the affairs of man.

Christmas

Christmas is a time of great joy. Traditionally, the Christmas season consists of twelve days and ends with the Epiphany. The liturgies belonging to this period are woven around the Matthew and Luke accounts of the baby Jesus.[3] The twelve days of Christmas (between December 25 and January 6) are important because they are festal celebrations of life. Specifically, they mark the celebration of Christ's life and the life He gave us.

The birth of Christ is the fulfillment of the Advent hope.

Epiphany

Epiphany was the first of the Christmas festivals and originated in the Eastern celebration of the incarnation.[4] Concerned chiefly with the revealing of God to the world in the form of Jesus Christ, the Epiphany centered on two things: 1) the birth of Jesus and 2) His baptism. All features of the birth were celebrated, including the visit of the wise men.

Epiphany means "manifestation" in Greek, in reference to the baptism of Jesus at which God revealed that Jesus was His beloved Son and He was pleased with Him (Mark 1:9-11).

In the East, the Epiphany was celebrated on January 6 until late in the fourth century. The Western world began celebrating the coming of Christ on December 25 in the early part of the fourth century. This spread throughout the East and became the time to celebrate Christ's birth. As a result, the Epiphany no longer commemorated the incarnation — only the baptism of Jesus.

Traditionally, two specific Scripture passages are read the two Sundays following the Epiphany: 1) the visit of Christ to the temple in Jerusalem at the age of twelve (Luke 2:41-50) and 2) the account of Jesus' turning the water into wine at the wedding in Cana of Galilee (John 2:1-11).

Today Epiphany is celebrated on the closest Sunday to January 6. It is a time for us to worship the Lord for revealing Himself to us and the world. It calls us to manifest Christ in our own lives to others.

Lent

Lent, which in Latin means "springtime," is a six-week period of spiritual discipline before Resurrection Sunday. It begins with Ash Wednesday. It has come to mean preparation for the death of Christ as well as the death of our own sins in Christ. We put away not just sweets or other favorite foods or activities, but all those things in our lives that need to die with Christ.

Lent probably originated when candidates were making final preparations for baptism at the end of Holy Week. It developed into a devotional preparation for all believers. Some practiced fasting for forty days (except on Sundays).

Liturgical churches observe the season of Lent as do some Methodist, Southern Baptist, Nazarene and charismatic churches. In this season we place our problems and weaknesses in the death of Christ. We worship the Lord in personal and corporate repentance. The themes of Lent are repentance, spiritual growth and entering into union with Christ.

Lent is a season when we can take a close look at our lives and examine our spiritual walk with the Lord. We can ask Him to show us things in our lives that we need to repent of. It can be a time of purifying our worship and focusing on the Lord.

Holy Week

The term *Holy Week* developed in the late fourth century. The celebration of Easter (or Pasch) became more elaborate at that time. It contained the lighting of the new fire of the paschal candle. A blessing was said at the lighting, and a song of praise was sung — the Exaltet. Then the vigil continued with teaching for the baptismal candidates (originally as many as twelve lessons from the Old Testa‑ment) on prayer and fasting. This gave way at the dawn of

Resurrection Sunday to baptism and the taking of the Lord's supper.

Holy Week centered around the Great Triduum, the three days from Thursday through Saturday evening.

Maundy Thursday

Maundy Thursday commemorates the events of the night Jesus was arrested. Some churches celebrate Maundy Thursday with a joyous *agape* feast, a common meal regularly held by early Christians for the purpose of displaying and growing in God-centered love. It emphasized spiritual fellowship with each other and the risen Lord. The Eucharist came out of this as the full meal slowly disappeared.

On Maundy Thursday, modern churches often also read the commandment which Jesus gave to His disciples that night, which was "to love one another" (John 13:34). According to *Webster's* dictionary, the word *maundy* comes through the Old French *mandé* from the Latin *mandatum,* meaning "command." It is associated with the ceremonial washing of the feet of the poor.[5]

Worshippers also experienced the washing of the feet and then celebrated the Lord's supper. After the service, the sanctuary may be left open all night for those who want to watch and pray as Jesus and His disciples did through that night.

Good Friday

From noon to 3:00 P.M. on Good Friday, Christians assembled to mark the time when Christ hung on the cross. Worshippers heard and meditated on the last words of Jesus. Later that evening, believers gathered again for the service of the cross.

Holy Saturday

Saturday was a day of prayer, meditation and fasting in preparation for the great paschal vigil. Of all the services of the year, this vigil was the most important. It is the source of all our worship because we celebrate the death and resurrection of Christ. Some churches today gather on Saturday night at 11:00 (or early Sunday morning at 5:00). The paschal candle is lit signifying the resurrection life of Christ bursting from the grave. Scripture is read, baptism is given to those who are prepared, and the Lord's supper is celebrated.

Easter Sunday was not celebrated in the first centuries as we know it today.

Easter

In the first-century church, the Easter celebration or Pasch (Passover) was a time of joy and celebration. It was a time to focus on the resurrection of Christ.

It became an all-night festival. During the time that represented the passion of Christ, prayer and fasting were in order. This was usually over Friday and Saturday. The Christian celebration of the Passover began on Saturday evening and ended at dawn on Resurrection Sunday with water baptisms and the Eucharist. As R. F. Buxton wrote, "It was in the light of the victory of the Lord's Day that the church looked upon the cross."[6]

By the third century the baptisms at early dawn were followed immediately by worship with the Eucharist. The baptisms occurred when fasting and prayer gave way to joy at the hour when Christ rose victorious over death. Those who were newly baptized then partook of their first communion. The celebration of resurrection joy was the highlight of the Christian calendar.

Of this time Augustine wrote:

These days after the Lord's Resurrection form a period, not of labor, but of peace and joy. That is why there is no fasting and we pray standing, which is a sign of resurrection. This practice is observed at the altar on all Sundays, and the Alleluia is sung, to indicate that our future occupation is to be none other than the praise of God.[7]

In the ancient church, the Easter season lasted fifty days. The preaching during this time pointed to the post-resurrection appearances of Jesus. The worship celebrated the presence of Christ among His disciples. It recounted the disciples' preparation to declare the kingdom of God. It ended on Pentecost Sunday, the day of the coming of the Spirit.

Pentecost Sunday

Pentecost Sunday was the celebration of the coming of the Spirit of the Lord. The Pentecost service is an opportunity for great celebration and noisy praise where believers glorify the Holy Spirit. The Spirit of the Lord should be summoned or invoked by the worshipper at this time as the disciples did according to Jesus' instruction (Luke 24:49-53).

The Value in History

The Christian calendar or church year is a valuable part of our worship today. Though abuses in the past led to its rejection by some parts of the church, special events can greatly enrich our worship.

In regard to using the Christian calendar, I changed my thinking when I looked at church history and saw how each holiday, or holy day, was celebrated in the early church. In the same way, I have learned about worship today by looking at how it has developed into its present form. ❦

15

SPIRIT-FILLED WORSHIP IN THE EARLY CHURCH

I N SCRIPTURE there is little reference to any set order of service in the church. The New Testament writers were more concerned with the principles of worship and with the spirit behind it.

It seems that the emphasis was on two things: togetherness of believers and unity of the Spirit. Togetherness of believers included physical proximity and the oneness of mind and heart. One historian observed:

> The dominating concern in public worship is to glorify God and to seek the welfare of the whole fellowship of the Church.[1]

They had purpose and a common pursuit — the oneness of the group and of the Spirit.

Believers were encouraged to give the Holy Spirit full reign in their midst, though they were to test the spirits. Everything was to be done in proper order. "Hymning" in praise was practiced and inspired by the Spirit of God. Believers were encouraged to be filled with the Spirit of God in order to sing songs of the Spirit (Col. 3:16).

The church in these early days flowed in a pattern of worship that was pliant and free under the direct supervision of the Holy Spirit.

In the next three centuries, worship became a little more organized — though by no means less Spirit-inspired — as recognized canons developed. We can discover a lot about the meaning of our worship forms today by looking at how they originated.

Justin Martyr

Most of what we know about the worship services of the second-century church comes from Justin Martyr (c. 100-165), who was known as the defender of the worshipping community. He was born in the Roman colony of Flavia Neapolis (ancient Shechem and modern Nablus) of pagan parents and sought to find life's meaning in the philosophies of his day, which brought many disappointments.[2]

In about A.D. 130 his life was transformed after talking to an elderly man.

> A fire was suddenly kindled in my soul. I fell in love with the prophets and these men who had loved Christ. I reflected on all their words and found that this philosophy alone was true and profitable. That is how and why I became a philosopher.[3]

Justin continued to wear his philosopher's cloak, seeking to reconcile faith and reason. His teaching ministry took him first to Ephesus (c. 132) and then later to Rome, where he founded a Christian school and wrote bold apologies addressed to Roman authorities. His first apology helped preserve detailed descriptions of early Christian worship.

In about 165, mostly because of his defense of martyrs in his second apology, Justin was denounced for being Christian. He refused to recant and worship with pagan sacrifices and was scourged and beheaded. He gave his life, the most costly worship he could give for this "true philosophy."

Justin did the church a great service by describing a Sunday worship service in Rome around A.D. 150. Following is a description of each of the parts of the service. You may be surprised to recognize many practices that are still in use today.

Reading Scripture

For as long as time permitted, "memoirs" of the apostles or the writings of the prophets were read.[4] It is most likely that the readings were consecutive, each one taking up where the last left off. The readings appeared to be rather lengthy, which is not surprising because they provided the principal opportunity for the average person to become familiar with the Scriptures.

Everyone stood during the reading of the Gospels. These books were the most precious of the New Testament writings because they spoke of the Savior.

Early believers were constantly aware that the Holy Scriptures were given by inspiration of God (2 Tim. 3:15-17) and would make a person wise unto salvation at the hearing of them. Therefore, Scripture reading held a central place in the order of worship in the early church.

There was a distinction between reading the Scriptures in a gathering of believers and reading them for private study. Paul admonished Timothy not to forget the *public* reading:

Devote your attention to the public reading of the Scriptures (1 Tim. 4:13, NEB).

The early believers read from the church's Bible, the Old Testament, but by A.D. 150 the New Testament had already reached canonical status, and the memoirs of the apostles were placed beside the Old Testament as authoritative liturgical documents.[5]

An educated and trained person would offer to read the Scriptures as a lector. At the hearing of the words inspired by God, the people would respond with an attitude of worship in their hearts.

In many charismatic, Pentecostal and evangelical churches, the public reading of Scripture is no longer practiced the way it was in the early church. I believe we need to return to reading larger portions of the Scriptures as an act of worship in itself.

Prayers

In the prayers of the early church there was an invocation of Christ as "sovereign" and as "supreme Master," based on Acts 4:24-30, and the title of Jesus was "servant." From the beginning of the church age Jesus was hailed in worship as One worthy of adoration and surrender and was placed at the center of the church's worship. Jesus was worshipped as the exalted Messiah and Lord.[6]

The Aramaic term *Maranatha* (see 1 Cor. 16:22) means simply "our Lord cometh." It had become accepted as a Christian prayer from the earliest days of the church and was spoken probably as often as we would say the word *amen. Amen* was also a very familiar Christian term. It was the people's wholehearted and full-throated response and endorsement of the words of another. It literally means "to be firm, true" and is connected with the verb *to believe*.

Another word often used in prayer by the early church was *abba*. It was our Lord's favorite designation of God. It means "dear Father."

There were times when early Christians said or sang free prayers that were spontaneous and individual. Justin Martyr said that they would "send up to him honors and hymns for our coming into existence, for all the means of health."[7]

Prayers would often begin with an address to God as Father and Creator and praises to Him for His mighty acts. From there they would move from thanksgiving to petition and close with a doxology — all being done with reference to Christ.

Standing, Kneeling and Bowing

On Sunday, Christians prayed standing because Christ had raised up humanity on that day. A sample early Christian prayer went like this:

> O God Almighty, who made heaven and earth and sea and all that is therein, help me, wash away my sins, save me in this world and in the world to come.[8]

There were many postures for prayer. For example, kneeling or prostrating oneself expressed humility, contrition, repentance and confession of sin. Standing, on the other hand, was a sign of joy and boldness, showing the freedom of God's children to come boldly into His presence. Standing also had a special reference to the resurrection and meant that the believer had a special privilege to come to God as Father, through Christ. To stand in the presence of God meant to be accepted by Him and to have the right to speak freely. In an age of bowing to emperors and kings, the privilege of standing in the presence of God was very meaningful.

Raised Hands

Believers would often pray with raised hands. Today we sometimes think of raised hands as a newer charismatic expression. However, Roman paintings and third-century frescoes clearly portray the posture of early Christians in prayer with hands and arms lifted. This was nineteen hundred years before the charismatic and Pentecostal movements. Lifting hands was simply a Christian act of prayer and praise in which all believers were urged to participate. Paul wrote:

> I desire therefore that men pray everywhere, lifting up holy hands, without wrath and doubting (1 Tim. 2:8).

Tertullian (c. A.D. 160-220) observes that this posture of outstretched arms was also important to early believers because it symbolized Christ on the cross. "We, however, not only raise, but even expand them [our hands]; and, taking our model from the Lord's passion [His outstretched hands], even in prayer we confess (or, "give praise") to Christ."[9] Some would also pray facing east, toward the Holy Land, in expectation of the Lord's return.

Singing

Singing has always been a vital part of Christian worship. In about A.D. 112, Roman governor Pliny noted in an epistle to the Emperor Trajans that Christians "met regularly before dawn on a fixed day to chant verses alternately among themselves in honor of Christ as if to a god."[10]

The following is a song likely sung by early believers.

Notice the theme of their celebration.

> Christ is risen: the world below is in ruins.
> Christ is risen: the spirits of evil are fallen.
> Christ is risen: the angels of God are rejoicing.
> Christ is risen: the tombs are void of their dead.
> Christ has indeed arisen from the dead, the first
> of the sleepers.
> Glory and power are His for ever and ever.
> Amen.[11]

Singing was often mixed with the reading of Scriptures in the early church. They would sing psalms or psalm-like compositions in between Scripture readings.

Singing was also part of their prayers. The prayers of the synagogue (a model for early Christian worship) were recited in a chant, and Christians may have followed that practice. The distinction we make between prayer (prose) and hymn (poetry or song) was not present in Justin's time.

The Sermon

The preaching of the sermon in Christian worship has its roots in the synagogue practice of exposition after the reading of Scripture. The sermon was expository, based on the Scripture reading of the day, and gave a practical application for the listeners. I believe expository preaching is more accurate than topical preaching.

A preacher should not dare to twist the Scriptures to fit the subject or circumstance of people's lives. Instead the preacher calls the people to bring themselves into subjection to the Scripture. The subject and emphasis automatically become evident. Our own particular opinions need not be announced. When the Word is exposed, it speaks loudly. This eliminates private interpretation or doubtful conclusions.

Sermons were based on the Gospels primarily, the Old Testament Scriptures and the writings of the apostles. Other writings were popular in Justin's time as well: the Didache (c. A.D. 125); 1 Clement (c. A.D. 95); and the Shepherd of Hermas (c. A.D. 112), to name a few. But none was considered authoritative.[12]

The sermon would be followed by everyone's standing up and offering prayers.

The Eucharist

At the conclusion of the sermon, bread, wine and water were presented for the celebration of the Eucharist. Two things were important about this celebration:

1. The consecration (dedication) of the wine and the bread. According to Justin, the wine and bread were set apart and given new significance when they were consecrated by the Word of God and by prayer (of thanksgiving).[13]

2. Receiving the communion. The communion elements were ordinary bread and wine that was mixed with water. They were offered to the Lord and then eaten and drunk by all those who were baptized. Justin referred to this act of worship as the Eucharist, which means "thanksgiving." The second-century Christians adopted this name.[14]

During the second century the idea of sacrifice began to be associated with the Eucharist. This is apparent in Justin's *First Apology* when he said:

For we do not receive these things [bread and

wine] as common bread or common drink; but as Jesus Christ our Saviour being incarnate by God's word took flesh and blood for our salvation, so also *we have been taught* that the food consecrated by the word of prayer which comes from him...is the flesh and blood of that incarnate Jesus[15] (italics added).

As Justin indicates, this sacrificial emphasis of the Eucharist had been taught in the church from at least two sources: the Didache and the prolific writings of Ignatius of Antioch.

The Didache was a two-part document (one part teaching of "the two ways"; the other part a manual of church order) written around the turn of the first century. This work called the Lord's table a "sacrifice" in light of Malachi 1:11,14.

Ignatius wrote at about the same time arguing forcefully for the Eucharistic sacrifice. He stated, in effect, that the Eucharist was not to be celebrated apart from a bishop and that the church was, in his view, "a place of sacrifice."[16]

As Ralph Martin, a scholar of early church worship, observes, these attributions would eventually lead to the full-blown doctrine of the Eucharistic sacrifice in the later church fathers.[17]

After the Eucharist the leader of the service offered extemporaneous prayers. The main theme was praise and thanksgiving to God for His gifts in creation and especially in redemption.

The congregational "amen" confirmed what had been prayed and signified that this prayer was the joint prayer of all those present. Justin was impressed with this element of congregational participation. This is seen by his description of the act with a word that has a double meaning: "to make acclamation" or "to sing." That word has been translated as "to sing out their assent."[18] It could have been a chant-like, unison acclamation. It was shouted out, not mumbled — possibly what some today call spontaneous praise. The congregation responded in a similar manner to the doxology.

Fellowship

Before the wine and the bread were brought forward, Christians would greet baptized believers with a "holy kiss" or "kiss of love."[19] This kiss was not ranked among those given by common friends. It was a kiss that would bind souls together and solicit complete forgiveness. This holy kiss was an expression of brotherly love and welcomed the newly baptized into the family of God. (No one could partake in the Eucharist unless they were in full fellowship with the church.)

The deacons would carry the consecrated elements of the Eucharist to those who were sick and unable to be present physically. This helped to preserve a sense of corporate fellowship among those confined to their homes or beds.

Offerings

Concerning offerings, Justin pointed out that "those who prosper, and who so wish, contribute, each one as much as he chooses to."[20] The early church gave offerings of produce as well as money. These gifts were voluntary, unlike the dues of the Hellenistic and Roman worlds.

The persons who benefitted from the almsgiving were orphans, widows, strangers, prisoners and the sick. The offerings were not left at the front of a religious edifice or idol as the pagans did with their offerings. The church supported those in need from the earliest days, as the Old Testament taught (see also Eph. 4:28).

Baptism

Baptism was a very important part of Christian worship. In third-century Rome a candidate received more than three years of teaching and was told that on being baptized he would be given more instruction. There was great anticipation as believers prepared for this special moment of worship.

Prior to the ceremony, the Christians participated in a fast and in a long session of prayer through the night in a dark building. By the flickering light of torches, they would exorcise the devil. Next the candidate would step into the baptistry.

He would then turn to the west and renounce Satan and turn to the east and confess Christ. Each candidate was anointed repeatedly with oil, a symbol of strength. He stepped down into the baptismal font until he was knee-deep. A deacon would put his hand on him and ask if he believed in God, the Father Almighty.

The candidate answered that he believed. The deacon then baptized him by pouring water over his head or placing his head under the water in the pool.

Once again the deacon would ask, "Do you believe in Christ Jesus, the son of God, who was born by the Holy Ghost of the Virgin Mary, and was crucified under Pontius Pilate, and was dead and buried, and rose again the third day, alive from the dead, and ascended into heaven, and sat at the right hand of the Father, and will come to judge the quick and the dead?"[21]

When the candidate said, "I believe," he was baptized again.

A third question was asked, "Do you believe in the Holy Ghost; in the holy church and the resurrection of the flesh?"[22]

The candidate again affirmed his belief, and the deacon baptized him a third time.

After coming out of the pool, the presbyter would anoint the candidate again with the oil of thanksgiving. The candidate was then brought out into the brightly lighted church and received his first Eucharist.[23]

Baptism was a serious step for a believer — denouncing the past, being delivered of demons and anointed with oil, and partaking of the Lord's supper. Perhaps we need to reconsider the important role the Lord's supper and baptism should have in our lives. Let's take part in these most cherished expressions of worship with more meaning and sincerity.

Models and Warnings

Worship in the first three centuries of church history provides great models for us to follow today. I believe that some of the resistance to learning from church history comes from what happened in the following years, particularly during the Middle Ages. The reasons behind this deterioration serve as an important warning for us today. ❦

16

SPECTATOR WORSHIP IN THE DARK AGES

I N THE fourth and fifth centuries the church grew rapidly, theology was formulated into creeds, and worship became more rigid.

When the Roman emperor Constantine converted to Christianity (A.D. 312), Christians found themselves in a radically different position in their culture. After A.D. 324, Constantine aggressively strengthened the churches and tried to eradicate paganism. Although Christians hesitated for awhile, they soon merged Christianity and Roman culture.

Constantine and his mother, Helena, erected buildings for Christian worship all over the Roman empire. Believers remained cautious, however, preferring to use the common public buildings, the basilica, rather than the Greek and Roman temples. As it turned out, when these grand edifices were used, they brought significant changes in worship.

The bishop had his own seat behind the altar, whereas in earlier times his seat had been among the people. It became a seat of power and honor and eventually a throne. This separated the bishop from the people, and worship was no longer centered in the congregation.

The church became more institutionalized, hierarchical and politically powerful. The bishop slowly became an authority outside the body of believers. Instead of being a servant of the body of Christ, he lorded over the people as his status was raised above theirs. These changes gradually reshaped the worship of the church.

Privileged Worship

Worship was once the work of the collective gathering of believers, but now it became the privilege of the clergy. The bishop and clergy were seated separately from the congregation, and the less-ranking ministers, singers and readers were placed behind them. They became a congregation within a congregation. The "common folk" were the farthest from the front.

The role of the common believer was to watch the drama of worship played out in front of him. This was a departure from the biblical approach to worship as an act of the people which required participation by all believers present.

This was more pronounced as the altar was separated from the people behind rows of columns (in the West) and by a screen with icons (in the East). The purpose was to increase the mystery of the gospel, but the result was to remove the action from the people.

The Eucharist was taken only by the clergy, except once

or twice a year when all could partake. This made the most sacred biblical act of worship remote and something that was feared and held at a distance. Early believers celebrated the Lord's supper every time they gathered. It was the highest act of worship the church knew and what they looked forward to the most. During the Middle Ages it was removed from the people.[1]

Christianity and Culture

The liturgy became more dramatic as the emperor became the number-one layperson in the church. Simple ceremony no longer sufficed. Processionals, lights, special dress and numerous other elements added to the grand setting to honor the emperor. Even the Bible was surrounded by rich ceremony that was meant to invoke awe and reverence for the Word of God. The Scriptures were carried by a deacon in a procession of ministers and followed by other people bearing crosses, candles and incense.

Did these efforts facilitate worship, or did they distance the believer from the Word? Did these changes help personalize worship or externalize and remove worship from the common man? Did this honor the Lord?

Popular culture was being combined with worship. But was there too much mixture of Christian culture with Roman and Greek culture? Should Christianity fit into any culture at any time and take on some of that culture's flavor?

By the end of the fourth century, Christianity had achieved a dominant position in the empire, and Christians felt they could borrow cultural language and ideas more freely than before.

Some Christian scholars say that early Christianity's adaptation to its culture was essential to its success. Like Paul the apostle, believers sought to be all things to all people so that Christianity might be the belief of as many as possible (1 Cor. 9:22).

Vast numbers of people came into the church after the conversion of Constantine. Even prior to that, around A.D. 260, there were about six million Christians in the Roman empire. This great influx made it necessary to develop a system of biblical instruction, the catechumenate, which helped to reshape the thought and behavior of all those attending public worship services. Overwhelmed by the numbers, the church soon shortened the period of instruction from three years to the forty days of Lent. The Sunday liturgy and the Christian calendar had to bear a heavier load for instructing the newly converted.[2]

The Loss of Music

One other significant change that occurred during this period was the gradual loss of music. The Romans in the first two centuries had developed large orchestras and choruses for state functions. The Greeks had little music tradition of their own. Their musical instruments and musical influence came mostly from Asia Minor and other Near Eastern countries. Their instrumental music became so identified with the licentious worship at religious shrines that it became almost impossible to use it for worship in the church. Therefore much of the church avoided it.

> The early Church fathers took the view that music is the servant of religion. They thought that only music which teaches Christian doctrines and disposes the mind to holy thought ought to be used in the Church. Believing that music without words could not do this, they excluded instrumental music from public worship at first.[3]

Some historians point out that the Council of Laodicea

143

banned congregational singing as well as orchestral music in A.D. 367. This had a strong effect on worship as the early church knew it. The congregation could not sing with what was being presented in worship. They were taking another step toward spectating instead of participating in worship.[4]

All worship music was centered around the trained singers who fulfilled the functions of the mass. Choirs chanted the psalms and sang canticles and hymns.

Once again, culture was proving to have a negative influence on congregational worship.

A Change in Meaning

It is important to note a significant change in the meaning of worship at this time. Two lines developed: 1) The established church increasingly emphasized worship as a mystery. 2) The monastic movement stressed the devotional character of worship.

Worship as a Mystery

According to Robert Webber, the idea of worship as a mystery has its origin in the mistaken use of ceremonial forms.[5] The problem was that the symbolic action or form was regarded as an end in itself. Then the action of worship became the mystery instead of what it represents — the gospel, which is the true mystery.

This shifted the focus of the worshipper off the Lord and onto the act of worship. No longer was Christ the center of attention or the center of worship.

The false mystery of the act of worship was further enhanced by the choice of language. Though the Germans, French and English became believers, the language of worship remained Latin. This gave mystery to the mass because many people did not understand the words of the worship service. This was a major blow to participatory worship. In many ways God was no longer the audience for the church's worship. The people became the audience; the bishops and clergy were players on a stage; and no one understood their lines.

The mass was emphasized heavily in the medieval church at the expense of other activities of worship. The Eucharist was no longer a celebration of one's salvation. Instead, it was taught that the Eucharist was the act of becoming saved. By the ninth century, Paschasius Radbertus presented the view that the presence of Jesus was in the mass because of the miraculous change that occurred in the bread and the wine.[6] This laid the foundation for the doctrine of transubstantiation.

In addition, the skill of expository preaching was lost.

> The sermon had fallen into a grave decline, most parish priests being too illiterate to preach; and the place of the Scripture lections had been usurped on a great many days by passages from the lives and legends of the saints.[7]

Much of the mass took on an allegorical character. The presentation of Christ was perceived mainly by the eye since the people could not understand what they heard.

In many cases the mystery was turned into superstition. It was believed that during the worship of the mass, souls in purgatory did not suffer, and, after mass, one would not die a sudden death. Real worship was lost by both the clergy and the people.

Worship as Devotion

The second line of thought about worship during the Middle Ages came from the monastics. Monks protested the worldliness of the church. They became a prophetic and influential movement within the church.

Originally they were not much different in their worship from the church. But as they developed their own approach to prayer, they saw it as the main content of life. Everything in life became supported by prayer. Prayer was the chief action of the monks.

This movement came in sharp contrast to the institutionalism of the medieval church. The monks emphasized the kingdom to come while the institutional church was the protector and sanctifier of the present world.

For the monks, worship became increasingly pietistic or devotional. Unfortunately, prayers eventually became a means to increase one's piety. Participating in the Eucharist was looked upon as a way to become holy — even sanctified.

A Terrible Toll

Worship as a mystery and worship as devotion took a terrible toll on Christians' understanding of the true purpose of worship, which is to glorify God. It's important to recognize how these misunderstandings of worship came about; we can thus prevent something similar from happening to us.

The Lord brought the church through this time of misunderstanding and began to reshape worship through a great man named Martin Luther and other Reformers. As you'll see in the next chapter, many important worship forms were restored. Yet they also introduced a lack of balance in some areas. Once again, history demonstrates some vital principles for the modern church to recognize. ❦

GOOD AND
BAD IN THE
REFORMATION

THE SINGER sings out of his revelation of Christ, and the writer writes from his revelation of the Lord. In the same way, the worshipper worships out of his theology. To bring about a rebirth of worship, the Reformers had to reshape theology.

Two changes took place during this period: 1) a movement away from devotion and mystery and 2) a movement toward understanding and experience.

The reform of worship at this time was not uniform. Some groups kept the continuity with the past, and others introduced new styles of worship. Yet there were concerns common among all the Reformers. They all rejected the mass celebration because they believed it had become a resacrificing of Christ. Luther charged that it had lost its original focus on thanksgiving and had become a propitiation to please God.

The mass had created other problems. People had been used to receiving all kinds of benefits from having mass — healing, release of souls from purgatory and other magical results. It became a legalistic means of buying salvation. The Reformers believed that this struck at the heart of Christianity, which was a religion of grace. God was pleased by faith, not by a legalistic act done for someone. The belief that the mere performance of mass automatically brought the presence of Christ required no faith on the part of the believer.

Bringing Back Music and Preaching

For a thousand years of Christian worship laypeople had rarely sung. Then came Luther. Luther loved music and gave it, after theology, "the highest place and the greatest honor."[1]

He revised the chants and chorales of the choir and commended the singing of hymns in the home after catechetical instruction. He also introduced congregational singing and wrote a number of hymns. This was a drastic departure from the passive worship believers had experienced up until that time. With the introduction of a contemporary music style, even the common man and the new convert could sing without being trained in the music of the church.

Even more significant in Luther's reform of Christian worship was the elevation of the sermon to a place of centrality. Preaching became a vehicle of salvation through the proclaimed Word of God. In the spring of 1523 Luther issued the following instructions concerning worship.

And this is the sum of the matter: Let everything be done so that the Word may have free course instead of the prattling and rattling that has been the rule up to now. We can spare everything except the Word. Again, we profit by nothing as much as by the Word.[2]

Overboard on Preaching

The Reformers insisted on the restoration of the Word to its previous place in the worship of the ancient church. This was a positive emphasis in that many came to know the Lord Jesus Christ as their personal Savior through the preaching of the Word. Yet at the same time people again settled into being spectators instead of participants because they were taught to sit and listen.

Preaching became highlighted at the expense of the rest of worship. The sermon was often the high point of worship in the evangelical church. Many again fell into the pattern of watching the clergy do the acts of worship although there was some participation in song. Involvement was not encouraged as it was prior to the medieval period.

This is important to see because it gives us an understanding as to how our worship services became what they are. It is no wonder there has been much opposition to the longer period of singing in contemporary renewal of worship. This attitude is as old as the Reformers' emphasis on preaching.

Until a few years ago, many church leaders considered music as just a preliminary. They showed their congregations that this part of worship was not important or at best optional by reading their messages during the singing or not even coming into the sanctuary until the music was finished. This represented philosophies of worship that were out of balance.

Ulrich Zwingli (1484-1531) went the furthest in insisting

that the Word was the only way to worship. He abolished organs as well as other music, vestments, pictures and anything else that would distract from the centrality of the Word of God.[3] This emphasis was most influential in the circles of Calvinism. Quarterly communion was the order of the day instead of weekly, though John Calvin was distressed by it. This influence spread among the English Puritans, Baptists, Presbyterians, Congregationalists and independents and spread across the Atlantic to American Protestant Christianity.

The Zwinglians considered all ceremonies as pagan and began to rid the church of all tradition. They were convinced that faith did not come through physical or external means but by the Holy Spirit alone.

Historical Does Not Imply Denominational

Some independent charismatics today sound a lot like Zwingli. They have not learned to appreciate the historical view of worship. Some believe that all tradition is to be abolished because it is part of the bondage of the denomination they came from. It must be remembered that the forms of worship we want to follow are historical — but not necessarily denominational. We should follow the forms of worship that Christ and the early apostles instituted.

By the seventeenth century the foundations were being laid for another change in worship. You can see what happened by looking at the distinct contributions that came from particular denominations. ❦

FORERUNNERS TO CHARISMATIC WORSHIP

THE TRENDS of worship from the seventeenth to the twentieth century were forerunners to the charismatic style of worship that we know today.

At that time, most denominations opposed liturgy, emphasized the Word of God and encouraged personal experience in worship.

In addition, the practice of field preaching and new songs of worship also influenced worship styles.

Avoiding Prepared Worship Forms

The Puritans began the anti-liturgical movement in worship, and it was further propagated by the Baptists, Congregationalists and Quakers. It was their premise that worship originates from the heart and does not begin from a book or other aid to worship.

John Smyth summarized it as an early Baptist:

> We hold that the worship of the New Testament properly so called is spiritual, proceeding originally from the heart: and that reading out of a book (though it is a lawful ecclesiastical action) is not part of spiritual worship, but rather the invention of the man of sin, it being substituted for a part of spiritual worship.
>
> We hold that seeing prophesying is part of spiritual worship: therefore in time of prophesying it is unlawful to have the Book (i.e., Bible) as a help before the eye. We hold that singing a psalm is a part of spiritual worship: therefore it is unlawful to have the Book before the eye in time of singing a psalm.[1]

These Congregationalists rejected the use of written prayers, believing that prayer should be from the heart, directed by the Spirit of God. They insisted that written prayers deprived people of their own thoughts and words. How could set forms of prayer or song meet the variety of needs in a particular congregation? They believed that set forms of prayer led to overfamiliarity and lack of interest. They went so far as to say that set forms were idolatrous as they equated the liturgy with the Bible. All of these points should be considered as we examine our contemporary worship.

Prepared liturgy or forms of worship that have a profound historical and biblical perspective can greatly increase the potency of our worship. But they should never substitute for the more spontaneous expressions in our worship that are more intimate and are personally relative to where we are at that moment.

In the biblical account of the apocalypse only two set forms of song are mentioned, the song of Moses and the song of the Lamb (Rev. 15:3). The rest of the vocal praise in heaven is probably spontaneous. It is what John called "a new song" (Rev. 5:9-10; 14:3). Those in heaven, the eternal state of worship, could use their own words and communicate their own thoughts to the Lord, very possibly as the Congregationalists proposed.

The Quakers focused on "waiting upon the Spirit" by every member of the congregation. They would invite the presence of the Lord into their midst and wait for the Spirit to speak to them. They also rejected any aids or liturgies in worship.

Worship was completely inward, which led the Quakers to reject some valid outward forms of worship. They reasoned that since they sought "Spirit baptism" they did not need water baptism. The Eucharist was receiving Christ inwardly, and, therefore, they decided they did not need to go through the external act of breaking bread.[2] The problem is that they did away with forms of worship that Christ taught the first church to practice (see 1 Cor. 11:23-26). Christ told us to eat the bread and drink the cup to proclaim His death until He comes.

The Quakers were one of the most extreme examples of the general trend to downplay worship through the Eucharist. However, most Protestants also limited their celebration of communion, often to only four times a year.

Bringing Understanding of the Word

A second trend of Protestant worship was a recognition that the congregation needed to understand the Word of God. Some groups, like the Congregationalists, read the Scriptures and commented on the meaning and interpretation of the text as it was read. Then the congregation would make prophetic statements or ask questions. The reading would be followed by a sermon that would run two or three hours with a break in the middle to stretch.

The Presbyterians emphasized expository preaching and practiced lecturing — making comments while reading Scripture. Ministers were to seek the illumination of the Spirit of the Lord in prayer and with a humble heart.[3]

Encouraging Individual Worship Experience

The third trend in Protestant worship was the emphasis on the individual experience of worship as seen in the Moravians, the Pietists and the Revivalists.

Among the Revivalists the place of worship was switched from a church building to the home. Free worship was emphasized as well as personal involvement in spiritual gifts. Morning and evening prayer was moved to the home, and the father became the minister to his family.

The Pietists stressed worship that focused on each individual's personal experience with God and not on the objective and corporate action of the body of believers. An ethical, personal walk with the Lord was propagated. This made it possible for less dependence on others for worship. Believers met in homes and prayed from the heart, and everyone shared and expounded on the Scriptures.[4]

Field Preaching

Field preaching began from a desire to see people converted to Christ, but it also served to influence church worship. In these services praying, singing and preaching had their own unique flavor. It was never intended that these services should replace public worship in the church buildings, but in some places they did. The style of the services shaped the style of worship in these churches. The worship was less formal and more lively, and the music was the type with which the unchurched could identify. Field services became the forerunner of mass revivals.

John Wesley was the most famous revivalist of the eighteenth century. He blended the Protestant forms of worship with the Pietists' emphasis on personal experience. He stressed the importance of conversion and personal experience (showing an influence from the Moravians).

Writing New Songs

The Revivalist hymns made a great impact on the reform of worship at this time. The mainline Protestants viewed hymns with great skepticism. Psalms and Scripture were the only expressions of song that the classical Protestant and Puritan knew. Hymns were very controversial because they were contemporary and had not been part of the church in the past.

> The notion that the church could write her own hymns of praise was an innovative suggestion that met with some suspicion. It was through Wesley, however, that hymnody became a mark of Protestant worship.[5]

The Moravians, earlier known as the Bohemian Brethren, contributed greatly to the widespread use of hymnody. The hymns were often on the subjective aspect of Christ's suffering. They were emotional and imaginative. They were written so that the worshipper would feel Christ's pain and therefore appreciate and adore the Lord.[6]

Pentecostal and Charismatic Worship

Pentecostal/charismatic styles of worshipping resulted

from these three trends in Protestant worship — avoiding prepared worship forms, emphasizing an understanding of the Word and encouraging individual worship experience — as well as the introduction of field preaching and new hymns.

Spontaneous expressions are earmarks of Pentecostal/charismatic worship. The service can be planned but must not be overly structured. Keeping an openness to the momentary direction of the Spirit is usually the mode of operation. Open worship as seen in prayer, singing of praise and the exercising of spiritual gifts is an important ingredient.

The tradition of being antiliturgical went too far by downplaying the Eucharist. It would be more biblical (Acts 2:46) and historical to celebrate the Eucharist more often than quarterly or even monthly. It may not be our charismatic or Pentecostal tradition of twenty or even ninety years, but it has been a Christian tradition for almost two thousand years.

Pentecostal and charismatic churches today have kept sight of the importance of understanding the Word through preaching, but they have also brought a sense of balance between that and other forms of worship.

Pentecostal and charismatic worship focuses on the participation of every member in worship. Understanding the gifts of the Spirit promotes ministry by individuals in the worship context. Body ministry, spontaneity and outward expressions of joy are some of the unique characteristics of charismatic worship.

Worship is congregational and corporate, yet personal and private. Some lift hands, while others shout as they are personally impacted by their Lord when they worship. Clapping, singing and praying with emotion and volume are often characteristic of this style of worship.

The Holy Spirit is also giving contemporary songs to the church today. Many mainline Protestants and some Pentecostals dislike them, just as their predecessors did. But that is changing as more and more churches which only used hymns are now singing contemporary songs. In the last twenty years there has been an unusual birth of songs in the body of Christ. Many of these songs that often come spontaneously in public or private worship have become part of our worship repertoire. The Holy Spirit is giving the church new songs for the rebirth of worship we are experiencing.

Now that we have a picture of where we came from, the question is: Do we know where we are going? Where does the Lord want us to go in our worship? I believe we should continually seek a rebirth of worship in our lives. I clearly remember the *second* time I had a rebirth of worship. ❦

19

A New Place
In
Our Hearts

I ATTENDED my first worship conference in Northern California in 1978. As I heard pastor after pastor explain what the Bible said about music, praise and worship, a metamorphosis took place in my spirit. I began to receive a revelation of what it was to be a worshipper and not just "do" worship on weekends. I discovered what it was to be a worship musician and not just a Christian musician.

It was my second rebirth of worship.

To attend this conference, I drove down from Vancouver, British Columbia, where my wife and I lived at the time. We thought our church was one of the few churches that really worshipped. We never would have said that out loud, but we thought it.

Our local church, however, wasn't the place for our rebirth of worship. The Lord spoke to us in another environment — in a new place. I believe there is a principle here that is valid in discovering worship renewal.

God told Abraham:

> Go to the land of Moriah, and offer [Isaac] there as a burnt offering on one of the mountains of which I shall tell you (Gen. 22:2).

Abraham was told to go to a new place of worship — a new mountain. He had to leave the comfort zones and travel to an unfamiliar place.

Sometimes we must go to a different place to discover a rebirth of worship. That is why youth camps, retreats and worship conferences are so renewing. At a worship seminar we get large doses of the Word of God for one or two days and experience the joy of worshipping Him in a different place. Together with other passionate worshippers, we can experience a fresh dimension of communion with the Lord. Our spirits are alert and sensitive as we assimilate what is going on around us in this new place. Jack Hayford says:

> We sometimes need to be pointed away from the worn valleys of our familiar ways to a mountain of God's assignment.[1]

Our worship tradition, our worship trappings and our worship forms are all securities to us. We become accustomed to them, and their familiarity kills our worship. We become used to them, and our worship becomes average.

Though it helps to be in a new location for a rebirth of worship, it is not a necessity. The core of the matter is to find a new place in our hearts. Let's look for a new place in our spirits and fan flames of love for Him that will grow into a passion for His presence.

Revitalized Hearts Bring a Rebirth of Worship

One of the keys to worship renewal is a spiritually revitalized heart. Lifting our hands, singing spontaneously or jumping with joy will aid in a rebirth of worship, but they do not make a nonworshipping heart into a worshipping one. The key is the condition of the heart.

Is your heart hot for the Lord? If so, then a rebirth of worship is just one step away. Simply stated, those who love God with *all* their hearts, souls, minds and strength are in a process of worship renewal. Those who find it difficult to give Him their worship without any preconditions are further removed from renewed worship.

We must live in His lordship to experience a rebirth of worship.

"Surrendering to God's claim is the core of worship," Jack Hayford writes.[2] God must have all of us. There can be no other gods before Him.

We cannot ask the Lord to renew our worship when we complain about the length of the worship. We cannot expect a rebirth of worship when we don't want to respond to a revelation of God with appropriate acts of worship. All of these things would point to a poor condition or focus of the heart.

A Heightened View of the Lord Brings a Rebirth of Worship

One of the most important ingredients to finding a renewed experience in worship is to heighten our view of the Lord. He does not change, but our view of Him is often not worthy of who He really is. We must think correctly about God in order to worship Him correctly.

We learn about the Lord through Scripture. We also can ask the Lord to reveal aspects of Himself to us so that we can worship Him with greater understanding. I like to read books that unfold the greatness and beauty of the Lord. Devotionals that deal with God's nature are excellent.

Another way to heighten our view of the Lord is to focus our songs on the grandeur of the Lord. They should speak of the kingdom of heaven, the rulership of the Almighty and the sovereignty and infinitude of our God.

Reading creeds or excerpts from the Psalms or the book of Revelation helps to heighten our perception of God.

New Songs Bring a Rebirth of Worship

Renewed worship requires new songs. The familiar songs that have become standards in our worship repertoire can be good expressions of worship. However, if that is all we sing, our worship could become rigid and cold.

Old songs bring remembrances of what God did in the past, even if they speak of the future. That's because our minds associate those songs with memories of what happened before. What is God doing today in your life? What is He saying to you now in your worship?

The lyrics of new songs unlock our understanding about the Lord in areas that we have perhaps not discovered before. They push the limits we have set in our worship and require us to grow spiritually.

New songs expand our worship expressions and open up new streams in our spirits. The Bible says that out of our bellies flow rivers of living water (John 7:38). These streams forge new paths for our expressions of praise to the Lord.

161

Spirit-Songs Bring a Rebirth of Worship

The most powerful new songs are not the ones we learn from other people, but rather the songs the Lord gives us to sing to Him. There is a uniqueness about singing a new song He has put in our hearts. When we sing these spontaneous songs to the Lord, the flow of the Holy Spirit increases in our hearts. Paul instructed believers to sing Spirit-inspired songs.

> Be filled with the Spirit speaking to one another in psalms and hymns and *spiritual songs,* singing and making melody in your heart to the Lord, giving thanks always for all things to God the Father in the name of our Lord Jesus Christ (Eph. 5:18-20, italics added).

These are songs the Spirit of God puts in us to sing in praise and thankfulness to Him. They are Spirit-songs. These songs encourage a rebirth of worship. They aid us in posturing our hearts to encounter the Lord.

I believe these may be the types of songs that are sung in heaven.

> The four living creatures and the twenty-four elders fell down before the Lamb, each having a harp, and golden bowls full of incense, which are the prayers of the saints. And they sang a *new song* (Rev. 5:8-9, italics added).

Heavenly choirs of elders, living creatures and overcomers also sang a new song.

> I heard a voice from heaven, like the voice of many waters, and like the voice of loud thunder. And I heard the sound of harpists playing their

harps. They sang as it were a *new song* before the throne (Rev. 14:2-3, italics added).

There is something powerfully refreshing when a congregation of believers lifts its voice in one mighty song of spontaneous praise to the Lord. Though there are a thousand melodies and an equal number of different lyrics, those songs are initiated and inspired by the Spirit of the Lord from the heart of every believer. In that kind of atmosphere it is easy to be renewed in worship and inspired to new realms of expression and communion.

Right Relationships Bring a Rebirth of Worship

A sense of community will also bring new life and vitality to a congregation's worship. It is important for a congregation to feel close to each other and in unity for the atmosphere to be conducive to a rebirth of worship. There is a link between what Christ has done for us, who we are as a people and worship.

The Scriptures tell us in 1 Peter 2:9,

> You are a chosen people, a royal priesthood, a holy nation, a people belonging to God, that you may declare the praises of him who called you out of darkness into his wonderful light (NIV).

We are a people who are part of Someone. We are not isolated individuals who only have relationship with our Creator and Savior. We belong to a group who, like us, have been purchased by His precious blood. We are saved to do something — worship together.

The church has gathered for two thousand years to celebrate Christ and the Christ event. The church as a community — a household of faith — brothers and sisters in the Lord come *together* to invoke the Lord's presence in worship. Perhaps you have noticed that when you have felt close to the members of a home care group, a Bible study group or a smaller church, you were able to get to some special moments in worship that were very meaningful to you. When we have warm, open relationships with those around us, we are better postured to encounter a rebirth of worship.

A sense of community is sometimes difficult in our Western society with our democratic mentality and spirit of individualism. But churches undergoing renewal are rediscovering the church as a *community*. Robert Webber notes:

> Without an understanding of what it means to be the church, believers run the risk of individualist worship, a worship that is not fully biblical nor completely satisfying to the soul.[3]

We do not worship in a vacuum. We worship out of community and in community.

Setting Aside Time Brings a Rebirth of Worship

We will not discover a renewal in worship if we do not allow time for worship. Putting a time restraint on our communion with the Lord is like looking at our watches when we are on a date with our spouses. No real closeness occurs.

We must allow time for worship privately and publicly — time for the Lord to speak and time for our response.

Being an Example for Others
Brings a Rebirth of Worship

Each one of us, whether young or old, can be an example to others in worship. In fact, each of us can lead others indirectly by our own exuberant participation in worship.

We have an effect on those around us when we give God praise with all that is within us. Those who want to be God-conscious, too, will be encouraged to get beyond their self-consciousness. The sparks of your passionate worship will set their hearts aflame.

Having a Rebirth of Worship in Churches

These are all principles that can be a part of a rebirth of worship in your life. But they are also aimed at a rebirth of worship in entire churches. The Lord has done a marvelous work in worship through the church. But I have seen some churches that have retained the form yet lost the Spirit.

As you experience a rebirth of worship in your life, don't be afraid to let it spill over into your church. A worshipping heart is contagious. And it's a good condition to catch. ❦

A REBIRTH
OF
WORSHIP

M Y LIFE was changed when I let this truth sink into my heart: The Lord *dwells in* the praises of His people (Ps. 22:3). He *loves* them. The place He chooses to inhabit is our praise and worship.

What gift can you offer to the Lord? The cattle on a thousand hills belong to Him, the earth and all that is in it (Ps. 50:10-12). But He is not the owner of your worship. You have the privilege of offering Him a gift that can come from no one but you.

My desire is that reading this book has made you uncomfortable. Wanting to change. Dissatisfied with the status quo — the familiar, the routine, the norm.

If you desire a heart of worship, you can have it. A heart that is warm, passionate and overflowing in worship can be yours. Ask the Lord for it, begin to implement some of the principles in this book, and watch the change.

> Dear Father, I realize You are searching for worshippers. Forgive me for my apathy in worship and my lukewarmness. Make my heart passionate for You.
> Let it overflow with vibrant worship. Empower me with boldness to give You wholehearted worship and to express the feelings inside.
> Help my worship not to remain intellectual and inward but rather become emotional and expressive. I commit the growth of my worship life to you. Bring me to full maturity as a worshipper who brings You great delight. In Jesus' name, Amen.

Take some time now and worship the Lord.

As you seek a new place in your heart for worship, remember the following principles:

- Be a worshipper every day of the week, not just when you're in church.

- Remember that worship is an attitude and an expression. Both factors are necessary for worship to exist.

- Recognize the call to worship that comes from the Lord, eternity, the Scriptures, your human nature and God's creation.

- Enter into worship during every part of the worship service, including the readings, the offerings, the singing and the sermon. A worship service means worship from beginning to end.

- Worship with all your heart, soul (emotions), strength (body) and mind (intellect and focus).

- Be willing to express yourself to the Lord through physical actions — dancing, kneeling, standing or lying prostrate.

- Embrace the awe and wonder of worship as you are captivated by His worthiness.

- Ask the Lord to reveal the purpose of His presence each time you worship.

- Make an effort to discern the good and bad effects of church tradition on worship. Learn from the good; reject the bad.

- Discover the Christian calendar as a way to focus worship on key events in the life of Christ.

- Learn new songs that will expand your expressions of worship.

- Sing "Spirit-songs" to the Lord.

- Set aside time devoted to worship.

I hope you find yourself discovering new expressions of worship on your lips throughout the day. May your time in the presence of the Lord be sweeter and more precious — your heart's greatest desire. I hope, too, that the Lord has given you a heart of worship. ❦

A MESSAGE FOR PASTORS AND WORSHIP LEADERS

A SIGNIFICANT metamorphosis is taking place in Christian worship that is both challenging and inspiring. It challenges us because it touches us in a fresh, new way. We must remember that the Lord is behind the transformation.

It is an awesome responsibility for us as pastors and worship leaders to navigate our congregations through changing tides of worship that challenge our comfort zones. Christianity is not a status but a journey. If we believe that we know all about worship, we have already become stagnant and have formed walls the Lord must penetrate to show us new things.

To bring the church to worship renewal we must be renewed ourselves in our worship. We must be the prototypes, models and examples of what God wants the congregation to be.

Motivation

What is our motivation in leading worship? Is it to bring people to Jesus and give them an opportunity to worship? Or is it to bring them to a certain emotional or spiritual place to accomplish our own goals?

Our objective as worship leaders should be a commitment to ministry, to help the people draw near to the living God. We must not "do" the worship for them, no matter how much the congregation applauds our efforts. Let the people worship.

A church often reflects us. When we flow with worship, the people sense the importance of it and do likewise. If we are not worshippers, the people will probably not be worshippers.

An entire congregation of worshippers needs no exhortation or coercion to worship, nor any promise of its benefits. There is little need for too many songs to help them focus on the Lord. At the first opportunity they simply lift up their hands and sing of their love for the Lord. In fact, true worshippers make opportunities to worship their Lord. Wouldn't it be wonderful to have a congregation of vibrant worshippers who overtake their leaders in their quest for the Lord's presence?

But it is also possible to have a worshipping leader in a non-worshipping church. It becomes the leader's goal to see the people experience that same passion for God's presence.

How to Lead Others to a Rebirth of Worship

Following are some principles that are keys to bringing the church to renewed worship.

First become a worshipper who pleases the Lord. I can't say often enough that as leaders we must be the worshippers God is looking for — those who worship Him in spirit and in truth (John 4:23). We cannot lead a congregation where we have not been. Seek a personal rebirth of worship. Ask the Lord to help you! We must be examples and pioneers for those who follow us. Too often vibrant worship does not occur in the church because the leaders of that church are not worshippers.

Develop a right concept of God. The acts of God, the benefits of knowing Him and how He meets our needs are emphasized among Pentecostal and charismatic ministries. These are all true and helpful; but focusing on them has compromised our worship, for then we focus less on who God is.

The Lord is our only audience, with each one of us being a worship priest, called to give glory to His name.

Have the people come to honor Christ? Have they come to give as much as possible to Him in worship, no matter what the cost? Do they want to worship expecting nothing in return? When this attitude prevails in the body of Christ, then worship becomes Christ-centered rather than man-centered, or humanistic.

"There is scarcely an error in doctrine or a failure in applying Christian ethics that cannot be traced finally to imperfect and ignoble thoughts of God," wrote A. W. Tozer.[1] This is a crucial area in our walk with the Lord.

What we think about when we think of God may predict with certainty the spiritual future of man and the future of our worship. To experience renewal in worship, we must have the right concept of God. It is basic to practical Christian living as well as to pure worship. It is as important to our worship as a foundation is to a building. Without it worship cannot stand. What church leaders think of God today will foretell where the church will be tomorrow.

Study about worship. Read the Word of God. Also read other books on worship by authors from various backgrounds. Some books to start with are *Worship His Majesty* by Jack Hayford, *Real Worship* by Warren Wiersbe and *Elements of Worship* by Judson Cornwall. They focus well on the essence of worship.

Develop a personal lifestyle of worship. Make a habit of reading God's Word and praying daily as well as offering the sacrifice of praise to Him continually. This should be done in our hearts and by our words. Singing a new song to Him as you move through the day will help keep your heart postured in God-consciousness.

As leaders we should be an example of the biblical revelation of worship we teach. David danced before the Lord as an example to Israel and led the people in whole-hearted worship. We should model what we want the church to be like.

Be real, warm and vibrant. We need to let the people see our humanness. Their response to us and our effort in pursuing God would increase if they knew we wrestled with the same problems they do. A broken spirit and a contrite heart will take each of us a step closer to a rebirth of worship.

Teach the congregation the biblical view of worship. Focus on worship's priority and significance. Let them see what God's views are concerning this subject and hear God's desire for their worship. Don't expect them to worship because you say it is important and necessary for every believer. Allow the Lord to impress them through His Word.

Other subjects to cover would be: What is the congregation's appropriate role or responsibility in a public worship service? What does God expect of them in worship? Show examples of Christ-endorsed worship in the New Testament. Teach worship in the life of Jesus. He is our example. We are His followers. What did His life of worship model for us?

To see the congregation become free in their expressions, study and teach about extravagant worship. Look at the woman with the alabaster box (Matt. 26:7). See how our worship needs no limits when the greatest commandment says to love Him with all our hearts. Jesus' triumphal entry into Jerusalem is another good example of lavish worship.

One significant worship topic is the purpose and place of the spontaneous song, or the new song. The understanding of this greatly aids a congregation in pursuing more Spirit-inspired worship. Showing spontaneous worship in heaven, in biblical history and in the revivals in church history is also very revealing.

Teach about the history of worship in the church. This will give those in your congregation from a Pentecostal or charismatic background a balanced perspective of the reformation of worship in the church. Their perspective is only a small part of what God is and has been doing in worship for two thousand years as He has been building His church.

Lead the people into the experience of worship. I'm referring to worship that goes slightly beyond the limits of the norm — leading people beyond their comfort zones into new territory in Spirit-led worship without hype or the help of our normal worship crutches.

Periodic and regular exhortations are good to enforce the priority of worship publicly and focus the congregation on the central issues of worship that have been explained. As the senior pastor, share your vision for what you want to see the body achieve.

Plan your worship services to focus on renewed worship. Ask yourself: What is the mission or purpose of the Sunday morning service? What are we as a church called to do? Developing a mission statement will sharpen the focus of the Sunday service and make it more effective in accomplishing its objectives.

I recommend writing down five things you believe the congregation is called to do in a particular service, such as teach the Word, heal the sick, preach to the unsaved, worship the Lord or reach out to the community. The first two priorities that surface will determine your mission statement for the Sunday morning service. Other services may have another purpose, such as being more seeker sensitive or geared for the uninitiated.

The mission statement of the Sunday morning worship service should spring from the mission statement of the local church. If it is to equip and train believers for the work of the ministry, then the Sunday morning worship service would have a similar mission.

Once the mission statement is determined, everything that goes on in that service should in some way fulfill it. The mission statement will tell you what parts of the service should be emphasized. For example, if your purpose for the Sunday morning service is to celebrate Christ with wholehearted worship, then the service would be planned with that in mind. The songs would focus on Christ more than on us. The sermon would lift up Jesus and not just give head knowledge. The offering and Eucharist would be Christ-centered. If the announcements did not serve the purpose of the mission statement, then less time should be spent on them.

Remember that sermons are a consequence and an act of worship. When preparing your sermon, keep in mind that a message from God is the living consequence of a vital meeting with God during which you worshipped Him. When the minister's study turns into a sanctuary, a holy of holies, then something transforming will happen as the Word of God is proclaimed.

We must not preach guilt. Preachers are not prosecuting attorneys but witnesses that speak of Christ. When we reveal God to people in our worship preaching, He convicts of sin. Isaiah saw the glory of the Lord and was only too willing to confess his sins.

Much preaching today is academic. We must explain and outline everything. Our tendency to analyze probably stems from the Greek worldview that operates in our school systems. When we do, we leave out the mystery that belongs to God and is a part of true worship.

When Paul completed his section in Romans on the sovereignty of God, he did not write, "There! I have explained it." He moved from writing to worshipping, from theology to doxology. Though he had seen many things, he did not feel compelled to explain them all. He concluded with:

> Oh, the depth of the riches both of the wisdom and knowledge of God! How unsearchable are His judgments and His ways past finding out! (Rom. 11:33).

When preaching is an end in itself, it is an idol before God. As R. J. Coates said,

> Preaching, if not sacramental, is profane. A true sermon is an act of God, and not a mere performance by man. In real preaching, the speaker is the servant of the word and God speaks and works by the word through the servant's lips.[2]

Keys to an Atmosphere of Worship

For every event of worship, there are several constants: time, space, players. As a worship leader, you must consider how each element contributes to leading others into worship.

Time: What day? Which service?

Believers have recognized that God set aside a day for worship.

> "Six days you shall labor and do all your work," Moses said to the people after he had spoken to the Lord, "but the seventh day is a Sabbath to the

Lord your God. On it you shall not do any work"
(Deut. 5:13-14).

God commanded the Israelites to set apart a day to think
on Him and worship Him — a day unlike any other in the
week. It was a holy day, a day of sabbath.

Sabbath means "rest." It was intended as a time of reor-
dering life and its relationships and values, which could
grow chaotic and disorderly during the previous six days.
So serious was this observance of time that there was a
biblical record of one family's being executed for violating
the sabbath commandment.

Biblical people were submissive to the time of sabbath.
They did not reduce worship to one or two hours on a day
when they would also mow the lawn, play football and catch
up on some of their chores. It was a day for the Lord — a
day to honor Him, talk to Him and spend time with Him.

For two thousand years most believers have worshipped
on Sunday morning. It is the morning of the resurrection of
our Lord. Since the church began, Sunday morning has
been sacred to believers. All the activities and worship that
occurred were only for Him. The services were never for
the outsider or for the believers — only for our exalted
Lord. It is my strong conviction that believers today should
continue to consecrate Sunday to honor the Lord.

So many congregations focus their Sunday morning service on the visitors. Though it is a very important consideration, it could affect our worship and compromise our
posture for a rebirth of worship.

When the focus of the local church is on the visitors, the
service will be planned to serve their needs and give them
the most attention. The songs are fewer, the message is
simpler, and the service is shorter. All of this is for the
benefit or service of the visitor.

It is important to minister to the unsaved and the uninitiated. But do we spend time with the Lord only if there is

time left after ministering to the visitors? The visitors may not want the attention. They may want to touch God's presence and be restored as they linger there.

Space: Do our surroundings affect our worship?

God meets His people in certain places or spaces. This conviction comes from Christ's teaching on worship to the Samaritan woman (John 4:21-24). Throughout history Christians have worshipped in catacombs, in prisons, in fields, by rivers, in homes and in the marketplace. Yet most believers have needed a *place* for worship — somewhere that could be set aside for the worship of the Lord Jesus Christ, dedicated to the glory of God and for the purpose of worship.

Houses of worship have contained the worship and the worshipper for millennia, and they are not a neutral entity. The design and appearance of a house of worship, whether it is an auditorium, a cathedral or a church building, convey something about the convictions of the people who worship in it. The principle of what we do in worship should be expressed in how we use the worship space.

Space belongs to God as the Creator, and it can be used to communicate. The outer court of the tabernacle, for example, contained both an altar for sacrifice and a large basin for washing, symbolizing the requirement of coming to God through salvation (sacrifice) and baptism (washing). The ark of the covenant was concealed in a room that held no other furniture, symbolizing the need to be focused and undistracted in our worship. Just the fact that much of Exodus and Leviticus is devoted to these instructions demonstrates the importance of space to the Lord.

Through the arrangement and appearance of objects in a church we communicate something, too — our theology. For example, if we have an empty cross at the front of the gathering place, it tells others we believe Christ is risen. If the cross has a figure of Christ on it, it declares that we are mourning His death. We may not believe He is risen; otherwise, the cross would be empty.

Throughout biblical history the Lord would inhabit space with His presence. He met with Adam and Eve in the garden. He met with Moses on Mount Sinai or in the tent of meeting outside the camp of Israel. The Lord met David in the space above the mercy seat on the ark of the covenant.

The act of consecration is important to space. It symbolizes the spiritual importance of the space in worship. Solomon dedicated the temple to the glory of the Lord, setting apart that space for the believer to meet with His God.

There was a certain space for the ark and for worship. Later, when the priest entered that space with the singers and players of instruments and began to worship in music, the presence of the Lord was very strong. The priest could not stand up and serve in his function because the glory of the Lord filled the space that was dedicated to and for Him.

This principle is unique and powerful, yet there is one question we should ask: Does the space in which we worship help or hinder our worship? The key is in the relationship that the internal space and the external space have in worship. One usually affects the other. What we believe and how we see the Lord within ourselves are reflected in the space that we dedicate to the Lord in the external, physical things around us. Our architecture reflects our theology. The believers' inward rebirth and revelation of Christ can be demonstrated by the spacial arrangement of the furniture of worship.

For example, if we believe God communes with His people, there will be furniture and space for activities that encourage intimacy with Him—altars, the communion table and so on.

When the meaning of worship is lost, then it is reflected in our use of space. We can see then whether or not we have lost the focus, function and purpose of worship. For example, when a church builds an auditorium to serve the needs of the platform ministry (such as high elevation; color lights; extra-powerful sound system and big monitor speakers; colorful set great for television; dark auditorium) and does not consider the needs of the worshipper, it may be communicating that what happens on the platform is more important. It may be a performance setting rather than a community worshipping. That will not facilitate worship renewal among the congregation.

Evangelism or preaching should not dictate the atmosphere of worship. Missions or youth ministries should not dictate the use of worship space. Only worship should. The building is called a house of worship because worship is the primary purpose for its use. The arrangement of the space should reflect that.

> Many sanctuaries are built as nothing more than auditoriums with brilliantly designed sound and light systems. Because we, as Pentecostals and charismatics, do not want to hint of any connection to traditional religion, so as to attract the "seeker," crosses, Eucharistic items, pulpits and religious art have been expunged from the architecture. And what is left to convey the reality of a holy place? Words. Words in song, drama and preaching.[3]

When God says that He inhabits the praises of His people (Ps. 22:3), the center of spiritual activity is among God's people — the worshippers. He did not say He would inhabit the praises of His priests or pastors or worship teams. The arrangement of space will reflect our beliefs.

I remember going into a very modern church that looked more like a public office tower. Some of the architecture gave a cold impression when you first entered. But when I saw the cross, my spirit was at rest, for this was where believers gathered to worship a risen Lord.

Church leaders should consider space in worship when choosing a new facility or designing a new building. What effect will it have on worship? Will it aid the believer in worship renewal? If the room is too quiet acoustically, it will hinder congregational worship. If it is too ambient, then communication will not be clear, and the sounds will run together.

From the earliest times holy spaces were set aside for what believers would do in the presence of God — namely worship. Altars were built there, and God was the focus. The arrangement of the articles of worship, the space of worship and the music of worship were to bring the worshipper to the Lord. The throne of God was exalted above the pulpit or the platform.

Players: Who should participate?

The main players on the stage of worship are the congregation. The pastors and worship leaders are the stage hands or the directors. God is the audience. Too often the directors and the stage hands get in the way of the players and do the worship for them.

Worship is for everyone. Often choirs, instrumentalists and singers hinder this by bringing attention to themselves. They seem to believe they are the players of worship, and the rest can participate if they are inclined. One step to worship renewal would be to ensure that all those on the platform are worshippers and understand that the Lord's attention is not on them but on the real worship players — the congregation.

Another question that comes to mind when we consider bringing people to a rebirth of worship: Do we lead worship by manipulation or by God-directed motivation? Do we as leaders sometimes leverage or hype the people to worship for our own purposes? We cannot make them worship or command or manipulate them to worship, for it is not worship then. It is only their active response to our ploy or maneuver. It is no longer worship because it does not begin in their hearts. If they simply do what we say, it may not be worship in spirit and in truth. We may feel good about our ability to get them to respond, but that does not make a good worship leader.

Is our worship man-centered? Do we worship to meet our needs? Do we worship as long as it is convenient and benefits us? What motivates us to worship? Are we self-conscious or God-conscious in our worship? Do we focus on ourselves and how we look or come across? Or do we worship the Lord with wholehearted abandon? Do we worship expressively, or are we inward and withdrawn in our worship?

Worship leading should not be relegated to the music minister because it is not a musical entity. Worship is not defined in Scripture as music. As shown in this book, worship involves so much more than singing. Because we as leaders are not musical, we are not exempt from leading worship. We know how to exalt the Lord and find His presence, so let's lead everyone there.

A Cry From the Heart

Many thousands of Christian leaders are coming into wholehearted vibrant worship. I have never witnessed such a passion among church leaders for the Lord's presence. Our worship is becoming the same in style, no longer so divided by older styles of our tradition. There is a blending and converging.

At a recent Worship Institute in Dallas/Fort Worth for evangelicals and mainline Protestants, many pastors came up to me with tears in their eyes. They appreciated the experience and revelation of worship because it was the cry of their hearts.

God has put that hunger in all of His body, and we must be His faithful servants to guard and guide that passion through. May we be the leaders of worship that will bring this generation into the vibrant worship reality the Father desires. 🍎

Chapter 1: Being a Worshipper

1. Walter Bauer, *A Greek-English Lexicon of the New Testament and Other Early Christian Literature*, 4th ed., trans. William F. Arndt and F. Wilbur Gingrich (Chicago: The University of Chicago Press, 1979), p. 338.

Chapter 2: The Living Heart of Faith

1. Philip Schaff, *The Creeds of Christendom*, 6th ed., vol. 3, rev. David S. Schaff (Grand Rapids, Mich.: Baker Book House, 1990), p. 676.

2. W. E. Vine, Merrill F. Unger and William White, *Vine's Expository Dictionary of Biblical Words* (Nashville, Tenn.: Thomas Nelson Publishers, 1985), s.v. "worship."

Chapter 4: Called to Worship

1. A. W. Tozer, *Worship: The Missing Jewel* (Camp Hill, Pa.: Christian Publications, 1992), p. 8.

2. William L. Holladay, *A Concise Hebrew and Aramaic Lexicon of the Old Testament* (Grand Rapids, Mich.: William B. Eerdmans Publishing Co., 1988), p. 223.

3. Don McMinn, *The Practice of Praise* (Irving, Tex.: Word Music, 1992), p. 21.

4. Charles Stanley, "Made for Praise," tape MD290, available from In Touch Ministries, Atlanta, Ga.

5. Jack Hayford, *Worship His Majesty* (Waco, Tex.: Word Books, 1987), p. 93.

Chapter 5: Worship Doesn't End With the Song Service

1. LaMar Boschman, *A Rebirth of Music* (Shippensburg, Pa.: Revival Press, 1980), pp. 28-29.

2. A. W. Tozer, *The Knowledge of the Holy* (San Francisco, Calif.: HarperSanFrancisco, 1961), pp. 20-21.

Chapter 6: Wholehearted Worship

1. W. E. Vine, Merrill F. Unger and William White, *Vine's Expository Dictionary of Biblical Words* (Nashville, Tenn.: Thomas Nelson Publishers, 1984), s.v. "prayer."

2. Francis Brown, S. R. Driver and Charles A. Briggs, *The New Brown-Driver-Briggs-Gesenius Hebrew and English Lexicon* (Peabody, Mass.: Hendrickson Publishers, 1979), s.v. "halel."

3. Graham Kendrick, *Worship* (Eastbourne, England: Kingsway Publications, 1984), p. 22.

4. *The Practice of Praise*, p. 95.

Chapter 7: Worship Him With the Dance

1. Merrill F. Unger, *Unger's Bible Dictionary* (Chicago: Moody Press, 1957), s.v. "dance."

2. H. M. Wolf, "Dancing," *The Zondervan Pictorial Encyclopedia of the Bible*, vol. 2, ed. Merrill Tenney (Grand Rapids, Mich.: Zondervan, 1975), pp. 11-12.

3. James Strong, "Hebrew and Chaldee Dictionary," *The New Strong's Exhaustive Concordance of the Bible* (Nashville, Tenn.: Thomas Nelson Publishers, 1984), s.v. "shûwar."

4. *Worship His Majesty*, p. 128.

5. *Strong's Concordance*, s.v. "râqad."

6. James Moffatt, *A New Translation of the Bible* (New York: Harper and Row Inc., 1954).

7. *A Greek-English Lexicon*, s.v. "skirtao."

Chapter 8: How Dancing Got a Bad Reputation

1. Jamie Buckingham, "Praise Him With Dancing," *Ministries Today* (May/June 1991), p. 47.

2. Ibid., p. 49.

3. Ibid., p. 49

4. Doug Adams, "Liturgical Dance," *The New Westminster Dictionary of Liturgy and Worship*, ed. J. G. Davies (Philadelphia: Westminster Press, 1986), p. 207.

5. Stephan Mansfield, *International Worship Symposium Manual* (Dallas, Tex.: International Worship Symposium), p. 200.

6. W. J. Hollenweger, "Pentecostal Worship," *The New Westminster Dictionary*, p. 431.

7. Buckingham, "Praise Him With Dancing," p. 49.

8. Ibid., p. 49.

9. Ibid., p. 50.

10. "Liturgical Dance," *The New Westminster Dictionary*, p. 208.

11. Buckingham, "Praise Him With Dancing," p. 50.

12. "Liturgical Dance," *The New Westminster Dictionary*, p. 208.

Chapter 9: Awe and Wonder

1. *The Best of A. W. Tozer*, comp. Warren W. Wiersbe (Grand Rapids, Mich.: Baker Book House, 1978), p. 179.

Chapter 10: Captivated by His Worth

1. *The Knowledge of the Holy*, p. 34.

2. C. S. Lewis, *Mere Christianity* (Westwood, N.J.: Barbour and Company Inc., 1943), p. 144.

Chapter 11: The Purpose of His Presence

1. *Worship His Majesty*, p. 48.

2. Ibid., pp. 53-54.

3. From an interview with David Kiteley, pastor of Shiloh Christian Fellowship, Oakland, California.

Chapter 12: Trends in Worship Today

1. Robert Webber, ed., *Music and the Arts in Christian Worship* (Nashville, Tenn.: Star Song Communications, 1994).

Chapter 13: The Rebirth of Liturgy

1. Robert Webber, *Signs of Wonder* (Nashville: Abbott Martyn, 1992), p. 3.
2. Ibid., p. 11.

Chapter 14: The Christian Calendar

1. Robert Webber, *The Complete Library of Christian Worship* (Nashville, Tenn.: Star Song Communications, 1993), pp. 418-420.
2. R. F. Buxton, "Advent," *The New Westminster Dictionary,* p. 1.
3. J. Gunstone, "Christmas," *The New Westminster Dictionary,* p. 171.
4. Ibid., p. 224.
5. Ibid., p. 367.
6. Ibid., p. 218.
7. Robert Webber, *Worship Old and New* (Grand Rapids, Mich.: Zondervan, 1985), p. 168.

Chapter 15: Spirit-Filled Worship in the Early Church

1. Ralph Martin, *Worship in the Early Church* (Grand Rapids, Mich.: William B. Eerdmans Publishing Co., 1964), pp. 134-135.
2. Cyrill C. Richardson, ed. & trans., *Early Christian Fathers* (New York: Collier Books, Macmillan Publishing Company, 1970), p. 228-229.
3. James E. Smith III, "Wordsmiths of Worship," *Christian History* (Carol Stream, Ill.: Christianity Today, 1993), issue 37, p. 28.
4. Early Christian Fathers, p.287.
5. Ibid., pp. 286-287.
6. *Worship in the Early Church,* p. 31.
7. Justin, "First Apology," *Christian History,* p. 13.
8. Ibid., p. 3.

9. Tertullian, "On Prayer," *The Ante-Nicene Fathers*, eds. Alexander Roberts and James Donaldson, Vol. III (Grand Rapids, Mich.: William B. Eerdmans Publishing Co., 1951), p. 685.

10. "Chanting in Honor of Christ" (*Christian History*), p. 45, quoting F. Forrester Church and Terrence J. Mulry, eds., *Macmillan Book of Earliest Christian Hymns* (New York, N.Y.: Macmillan Books, 1988).

11. Ibid.

12. *Early Christian Fathers*, pp. 15, 232-233.

13. Ibid., p. 286.

14. Ibid., pp. 285-286.

15. Ibid., p. 286.

16. "Ignatius, Smyrnaeus, 8; Magnesians, 7:2; Philadelphians, 4," *The Epistles of St. Clement of Rome and St. Ignatius of Antioch*, trans. James A. Kleist (Westminster, Md.: Newman Book Shop, 1946).

17. *Worship in the Early Church*, p. 139.

18. *Early Christian Fathers*, pp. 285-286.

19. Ibid., pp. 285-286.

20. Ibid., p. 287.

21. "An Awe-Inspiring Ceremony," *Christian History*, p. 41.

22. Ibid.

23. Ibid.

Chapter 16: Spectator Worship in the Dark Ages

1. *Worship Old and New*, p. 156-158.

2. E. Glenn Hinson, "Worshipping Like Pagans," *Christian History*, p. 20.

3. Frank Longino, *The Orchestra in Worship* (Mobile, Ala.: Selah Music Ministries, 1987), p. 23.

4. Ibid., p. 23.

5. *Worship Old and New*, p. 67.

6. Ibid., p. 68.

7. William D. Maxwell, *An Outline of Christian Worship* (London: Oxford University Press, 1939), p. 72.

Chapter 17: Good and Bad in the Reformation

1. James E. Smith III, "Wordsmiths of Worship," *Christian History*, p. 28.

2. Martin Luther, "Concerning the Order of Public Worship," *Luther's Works: Liturgy and Hymns,* eds. Ulrich S. Leupold and Hulmut T. Lehmann (Philadelphia: Fortress Press, 1965), p. 14.

3. *Worship Old and New,* p. 159.

Chapter 18: Forerunners to Charismatic Worship

1. Davies, "Baptist Worship," *The New Westminster Dictionary of Worship,* p. 90ff.

2. Davies, "Quaker Worship," *The New Westminster Dictionary of Liturgy and Worship,* pp. 328-329.

3. *Worship Old and New,* p. 81.

4. Ibid., p. 82.

5. Ibid.

6. Ibid.

Chapter 19: A New Place in Our Hearts

1. Jack Hayford, *The Heart of Praise* (Ventura, Calif.: Regal Books, 1961), p. 18.

2. Ibid., p. 18.

3. *Signs of Wonder,* p. 64.

Appendix: A Message for Pastors and Worship Leaders

1. *The Knowledge of the Holy,* p. 2.

2. Warren Wiersbe, *Real Worship* (Nashville, Tenn.: Thomas Nelson, 1986), p. 121.

3. Gordon MacDonald, "The Constants of Worship," *Worship Leader* Magazine (October/November 1992), p. 27.

BIBLIOGRAPHY

Bauer, Walter. *A Greek-English Lexicon of the New Testament and Other Early Christian Literature.* 4th ed. Translated, adapted and augmented by William F. Arndt and F. Wilbur Gingrich. 2nd ed. Revised from Walter Bauer's 5th ed. by F. Wilbur Gingrich and Frederick W. Danker. Chicago: The University of Chicago Press, 1979.

Bromiley, Geoffrey W., ed. *The International Standard Bible Encyclopedia.* rev. ed., vols. 1-4. Grand Rapids, Mich.: William B. Eerdmans Publishing Co., 1986.

Brown, Colin, ed. *Dictionary of New Testament Theology.* Vols. 1-3. Grand Rapids, Mich.: Zondervan Publishing House, 1986.

Brown, Francis, S. R. Driver and Charles A. Briggs, eds. *The New Brown-Driver-Briggs-Gesenius Hebrew and English Lexicon.* Peabody, Mass.: Hendrickson Publishers, 1979.

Cornwall, Judson. *Elements of Worship.* South Plainfield, N.J.: Bridge Publishing, 1985.

———. *Let Us Worship.* South Plainfield, N.J.: Bridge Publishing, 1983.

Davies, J. G., ed. *The New Westminster Dictionary of Liturgy and Worship.* Philadelphia: The Westminster Press, 1986.

Hayford, Jack W. *The Heart of Praise.* Ventura, Calif.: Regal Books, 1992.

———. *Worship His Majesty.* Waco, Tex.: Word Books, 1987.

Holladay, William L. *A Concise Hebrew and Aramaic Lexicon of the Old Testament.* Grand Rapids, Mich.: William B. Eerdmans Publishing Co., 1988.

Kendrick, Graham. *Worship*. Eastbourne, England: Kingsway Publications, 1984.

Kittel, Gerhard and Gerhard Friedrich, eds. *Theological Dictionary of the New Testament*. Translated and abridged in one volume by Geoffrey W. Bromiley. Grand Rapids, Mich.: William B. Eerdmans Publishing Co., 1985.

Longino, Frank. *The Orchestra in Worship*. Mobile, Ala.: Selah Music Ministries, 1987.

Martin, Ralph P. *Worship in the Early Church*. Grand Rapids, Mich.: William B. Eerdmans Publishing Co., 1964.

MacArthur, John, Jr. *The Ultimate Priority*. Chicago, Ill.: Moody Press, 1960.

McMinn, Don. *Entering His Presence*. South Plainfield, N.J.: Bridge Publishing, 1986.

———. *The Practice of Praise*. Irving, Tex.: Word Music, 1992.

———. *A Heart Aflame!* Oklahoma City, Okla.: NCM Press, 1993.

Mitman, F. Russell. *Worship Vessels*. San Francisco, Calif.: Harper and Row, 1987.

Tozer, A. W. *The Knowledge of the Holy*. New York, N.Y.: HarperSanFrancisco, 1961.

Vine, W. E., Merrill F. Unger and William White. *Vine's Expository Dictionary of Biblical Words*. Nashville: Thomas Nelson Publishers, 1985.

Webber, Robert E. *Signs of Wonder*. Nashville, Tenn.: Abbott Martyn, 1992.

———. *Worship Is a Verb*. Waco, Tex.: Word Books, 1985.

Wiersbe, Warren W. *Real Worship*. Nashville, Tenn.: Oliver Nelson, 1986.

For more information on other worship books,
videos and cassettes by LaMar Boschman, write:

LaMar Boschman Ministries
P. O. Box 130
Bedford, TX 76095

Other books include:

A Rebirth of Music (English and Spanish)
The Prophetic Song (English and Spanish)
A Passion for His Presence

The International Worship Leaders' Institute

The worship institute is a training center for all believers
including pastors, worship leaders and musicians.
From its beginning in 1986, the institute has been
designed to equip in the theology,
philosophy and experience of worship.

Its goal is to help train and equip church
leaders to lead others more effectively into the
presence of God. This is one of the greatest
opportunities available to worship teams today.

Speakers in the past have included Judson Cornwall,
Bob Fitts, Steve Fry, Bob Sorge, Joseph Garlington,
Phil Driscoll, Gerrit Gustafson, Andy Park
and Charles Simpson.

For a brochure, please write:

International Worship Leaders' Institute
P. O. Box 130
Bedford, Texas 76095

If you enjoyed *A Heart of Worship,* we would like to recommend the following books:

Silencing the Enemy
by Robert Gay

Praise and worship are more than words and music. They are a weapon of warfare. Robert Gay will teach you what God's Word says about the power of praise to break down strongholds, bring healing and deliverance and release prophetic messages.

Passion for Jesus
by Mike Bickle

Bickle shares from his own life experiences what it means to be consumed with the personality of God. This contagious message will bring you into a new and exciting life and help you gain an extravagant love for God.

Public Praise
by Graham Kendrick

Graham Kendrick's powerful book will motivate you to flood your life and your city with praise and prayer. This book explains the spiritual dynamics of praise marching and chronicles the beginnings of what could be one of the most significant movements of our generation.

Available at your local Christian bookstore or from:

Creation House
600 Rinehart Rd.
Lake Mary, FL 32746
1-800-283-8494